CATHOLICS AND FUNDAMENTALISTS

UNDERSTANDING AND RESPONSE

CATHOLICS AND FUNDAMENTALISTS

UNDERSTANDING AND RESPONSE

Revised Edition

Rev. Martin Pable

PUBLICATIONS

CATHOLICS & FUNDAMENTALISTS
Understanding and Response, Revised Edition
by Martin Pable, OFM Cap.

Edited by Andrew Yankech
Cover Design by Tom A. Wright
Text Design and Typesetting by Patricia A. Lynch

Scripture quotations are from the *New Revised Standard Version Bible*, copyright © 1989 by the Division of Christian Education of the National Council of the Churches of Christ in the USA. Used by permission.

Published by ACTA Publications, 5559 W. Howard Street, Skokie, IL 60077-2621, (800) 397-2282, www.actapublications.com

Library of Congress Number: 2007939187

ISBN: 978-0-87946-167-6

Printed in the USA by Versa Press

Year 16 15 14 13 12 11 10 09 08
Printing 10 09 08 07 06 05 04 03 02 01

CONTENTS

INTRODUCTION

In the years since the Second Vatican Council, Catholics have been working hard to further the process of Church renewal. Dramatic changes in the liturgy, new approaches to religious education, greater participation of the laity in parish administration and ministry have all moved forward in spite of fears, mistakes, uncertainties and resistances. Yet just when these efforts seemed to be bearing fruit, a new phenomenon burst upon Catholics: the challenge of fundamentalism.

Fundamentalist Protestant Christian churches continue to draw numerous Catholics into their ranks. Some claim that as many as fifty to seventy percent of these churches are made up of former Catholics. There is clearly a powerful energy here that demands some kind of response on the part of Catholics besides casual indifference or helpless hand wringing. I often say that if you had a business that was losing one-fourth to one-third of its customers to a competitor, would you not try to understand why and take some corrective action?

In addition, recent times have witnessed the rise of other forms of religious fundamentalism. The most visible is Islamic fundamentalism, with its violent demands for spreading a strict form of the religion of Muhammad, by force if necessary. But even within the Catholic Church there appears to be a group of people who exhibit fundamentalist tendencies; that is, they claim to have all the answers and seek to impose them on everyone else.

For these reasons, it seemed opportune to publish a new edition of this book, which first appeared in 1991. The present volume includes material from earlier editions, as well as much that is new. I have tried to present a fair and balanced picture of fundamentalism, whether Protestant, Muslim or Catholic. Aimed primarily at practicing Catholics, especially those who have questions about fundamentalist teachings and mainline Catholic responses to those teachings, this book was also written in the hope that some fundamentalist readers may be disposed to look at both sides of the questions raised here with an open mind.

Finally, it is my personal hope that Catholics who read this book will discover a deeper appreciation of their own faith and develop greater confidence in their ability to explain their beliefs to friends, family members and co-workers.

WHAT IS FUNDAMENTALISM?

My earlier work on fundamentalism was designed to help Catholics understand and respond to criticisms leveled at them from fundamentalist Christians. Since then, however, the phenomenon of fundamentalism has spread far beyond that particular tension. Most striking has been the rise of Islamic fundamentalism, which is often blamed for terrorist attacks and hate speeches directed at Western nations, particularly the United States. Some observers have also noted a certain fundamentalism among some Catholics who insist that only their beliefs and practices (especially liturgical) have the true mark of orthodoxy.

One of the purposes of this volume is to take a broader look at fundamentalism as it is manifested in today's society and how it affects many besides Catholics. Before proceeding any further, then, we need to define what we are talking about. I would like to propose the following definition of fundamentalism as the one I will use throughout this book:

> fundamentalism: *a set of religious beliefs that moves the believer to reject all contrary beliefs and to attempt to convert others to the fundamentalist belief system*

This definition is deliberately broad, so as to include a plurality of forms of fundamentalism. Note that the first element is a set or cluster of religious beliefs—about the nature of God, human beings, and the universe—presumed to be divinely revealed. Moreover, this set of beliefs is exclusive; that is, it does not allow for the existence of contrary religious beliefs.

So far, this definition could apply to almost any group of religious adherents. What makes fundamentalism unique is two other distinct marks. First, f*undamentalism implies a certain intolerance*. Again, all religions may be said to be intolerant in the sense that they hold their belief system to be the only completely true one. Yet most religions also respect the rights of others to believe and practice a different faith. For fundamentalists, however, such tolerance is categorically incompatible with their belief system. If their faith is the one true faith, all others must be false and should not be tolerated.

This leads us to the second mark of fundamentalism: *Fundamentalism implies a militancy that goes beyond normal and acceptable limits*. Many fundamentalists believe that if their faith is the only true one, then they have a mission to convert nonbelievers and bring them into the truth—the truth as understood by the fundamentalists. This is often done under the banner of "saving" people or preventing them from eternal damnation by insuring that they go to heaven. While it is true that most religions have a missionary or evangelizing aspect (the belief that faith should be shared with others), the difference lies in the intensity and methods with which fundamentalists pursue this aspect of their faith. Protestant fundamentalists will pressure—through friendliness, guilt, fear of going to hell—unbelievers and even other Christians to forsake their "evil" way of life and find salvation in the fundamentalist church. Islamic fundamentalists will embrace the notion of "jihad," a form of spiritual warfare, to impose their form of Islam on others, including other Muslims. Catholic fundamentalists will denounce other Catholics as being unorthodox and demand that their bishop or the Vatican rein in those they consider too radical, or even excommunicate them.

There is one other problem with a fundamentalist approach to religion: *Fundamentalism lacks a historical perspective*. Protestant fundamentalists often talk as if there was no Christianity before the Reformation; and some seem unaware of the great sixteenth century Catholic reformers such as Francis and Clare of Assisi, Dominic, and others. They act as if there was some "great awakening" to Christ somewhere in the last century or two and no one had ever been a believer before them. Islamic fundamentalists likewise show no awareness of the long history of their religion and its centuries of peaceful coexistence with Jews and Christians. Catholic fundamentalists speak as if the church existed from the very beginning in the form they experienced it in the 1950s; they seem unaware of how much and how often the church has changed throughout history.

Let's be clear: One can admire the energy, devotion, and passion with which fundamentalists practice their religion and try to propagate it, without joining their ranks or adopting their methods. In some ways the passion of fundamentalists is a refreshing contrast to the casual, laid-back, half-hearted, anything-goes mentality of many religious people today. At the same time, however, fundamentalism can be a dangerous form of religious zealotry. It forms the basis for the ideology that drove the Roman persecution of Christians, the Catholic persecution of Jews and Muslims, the excesses of the Crusades and the Inquisition, the Muslim "holy wars," and the Puritan witch hunts. It is the fundamentalist ideology that gives religion a bad name in every generation.

Origins of Fundamentalism

Fundamentalism is not the same as traditionalism or conservatism. These tendencies are present in every major religion. Modern Protestant fundamentalism began as a reaction to major intellectual upheavals in the late nineteenth century. In biology, the evolutionary theory of Charles Darwin seemed to contradict the biblical accounts of creation by postulating that the earth gradually evolved over a period of billions of years and that humans themselves have evolved from lower forms of life. In psychology, Sigmund Freud claimed that human freedom of the will is an illusion, that our choices are really determined by unconscious motives buried deep in our psyche. And Karl Marx maintained that religion is a creation of the ruling classes to control the working class and the poor: "Don't worry if you have to suffer in this life; you will be rewarded in the life to come." He dismissed religion as "the opium of the people," a drug to dull them to their oppression by the upper classes.

In response to these attacks on traditional religion, some liberal Protestant scholars tried to make some accommodation to the new scientific thinking. They began to study the Bible more critically, taking into account the various literary forms in which the Bible was written, as well as the findings of archaeology and cultural anthropology. They concluded that not all biblical accounts had to be understood literally, that evolution did not necessarily contradict the Scriptures, and that some of the biblical truths were open to various interpretations.

Understandably, this kind of thinking created a reaction in the minds of many Christian believers. Between the years 1910 and 1915, some conservative Protestant scholars wrote a series of booklets called *The Fundamentals*. In the series they rejected the "modernist" attempt to accommodate Christian teaching to the claims of science. They insisted on adherence to a number of doctrinal points, the main ones being:

- the absolute inspiration and inerrancy of the words of the Bible
- . the virginal birth and divinity of Jesus Christ
- the substitutionary atonement for our sins through Christ's death on the cross
- the bodily resurrection of Christ
- the literal Second Coming of Christ at the end of time

Since their publications, the first and third of these "fundamentals" have come to characterize modern Protestant fundamentalism. Because the Bible is the inspired and infallible word of God, it must be accepted as the sole norm of religious belief and practice. Knowingly or not, fundamentalists have appropriated one of Martin Luther's most famous "protests": *sola Scriptura.* They believe that "the Bible alone" is the source of truth for Christians. There is no need for any church authority or hierarchy to mediate God's truth to the faithful. They will be guided simply by reading or hearing the Scriptures and allowing God's word to touch the mind and heart. Moreover, there is no need for anyone to "explain" or "interpret" the Bible, because it is clear and easy to understand. Fundamentalists are fond of quoting one of their own scholars, Charles Hodge: "The Bible is a plain book. It is intelligible by the people. And they have the right and are bound to read and interpret it for themselves; so that their faith may rest on the testimony of the Scriptures, and not that of the Church."

> *Knowingly or not, fundamentalists have appropriated one of Martin Luther's most famous "protests":* sola Scriptura. *They believe that "the Bible alone" is the source of truth for Christians.*

As for the third fundamental, Protestant fundamentalism focuses on the personal acceptance of Jesus Christ as Lord and Savior. They believe that since we are utterly unable to atone for our sins our only hope is to trust in the redemptive death of Jesus on the cross for our sins (substitutionary atonement). This requires of the believer a deeply personal act of surrender and confidence in the power of Christ to save. Hence the defining question fundamentalists ask: "Have you been saved?" or "Do you accept Jesus Christ as your personal Lord and Savior?" In his now classic work *Catholicism and Fundamentalism*, Karl Keating expands on this notion:

This is unalloyed Christian individualism. The individual is saved without regard to a church, the congregation, or anyone else. It is a one-to-one relationship, with no mediators, no sacraments, just the individual Christian and his Lord. The Christian knows when he has been saved, down to the hour and minute of his salvation, because his salvation came when he "accepted" Christ. It came like a flash, never to be forgotten, the way it came to Paul on the Damascus road. (p. 23)

Keating goes on to note how this dynamic explains the evangelism of fundamentalists. If others do not undergo the same kind of salvation experience, they will go to hell. It is a matter of charity (and urgency) to save people from such a fate; so fundamentalists have a duty to spread their faith and convert others to it.

It should be noted that the mainline Protestant churches (Lutheran, Methodist, Presbyterian, etc.) do not hold to the fundamentalist theology described above, at least in its rigid form. The doctrines and practices we have noted are generally found in churches like the Assemblies of God, Community Churches, Bible Churches, and Pentecostal Churches. Some also describe themselves as "nondenominational" churches. In recent years they have shown remarkable growth, and tend to attract large numbers, especially former Roman Catholics. We will return to this phenomenon later.

❈ ❈ ❈

We turn now to the origins of Islamic fundamentalism. The founder and central figure of the Islamic faith is the prophet Muhammad. Beginning in the year 610 he received a number of revelations from God and were transcribed into the Qur'an, the Islamic holy book. Over generations, statements and actions attributed to Muhammad and transmitted orally by his followers were collected and written down as hadiths, something like oral traditions. Together with the Qur'an and the consensus of learned Muslim scholars, they form the sharia, Islam's sacred law. (Much of the following is based on material from *Islamic Fundamentalism: A Brief Survey* by Bruce Gourley and from Islam: A Primer by Clyde Mark).

After Muhammad's death, the community broke into rival factions over leadership. Eventually they evolved into what we know today as Shiites and Sunnis. There are fundamentalist tendencies in both groups, but they are more common among Sunnis. By the end of the ninth century Sunnis had established the Hanbali school of law, which held to the Qur'an as the literal, unquestioned Word of God. In the eighteenth century in Arabia, the Hanbali tradition gave rise to the strict Wahabbi school of Islam. The Wahabbis believed that modern Islam had become corrupted and polluted from within, and sought to return Islam to its pure roots. The movement became very influential, leading to the founding of other similar reform movements. In the twentieth century, Wahabbi Islam would provide the theological foundation for a political fundamentalist state, as exemplified in present-day Saudi Arabia.

The shift from revivalism to fundamentalism initially took place through the Egyptian Muslim Brotherhood movement in the 1930s. Founded in 1929 by Hassan al-Banna, the Muslim Brotherhood tapped into popular unrest against British rule, local political turmoil, and the corrupting influence of the West. Al-Banna's movement was based on the Qur'an and the hadiths, and it translated doctrine into social action at a time when Egypt was in social unrest. The Brotherhood initially espoused nonviolence, but gradually took up violent action, especially after the assassination of al-Banna. A crucial event was the victory of Israel in the Six-Day War in 1967. Islamic fundamentalists claimed that the Arab world lost the war because of lack of religious faith. They called for the imposition of Islamic law (*sharia*) in Muslim nations and communities. When Anwar Sadat became president of Egypt in 1970, he established Islam as the official religion of the Egyptian state, and sharia law as the main source of legislation. However, Sadat's openness to the West and to Israel was scorned by the multiplying Islamic fundamentalist organizations. In September of 1981, he led the government in taking direct control of all mosques and arresting thousands of militants. One month later, he was assassinated by members of the Islamic fundamentalist group Tanzim-al-Jihad.

While the vast majority of Muslims are content to practice their religion freely without trying to impose it on others, there is a fundamentalist wing that, at the very least, wants all Muslims to conform to Islamic laws, including prayer, diet, dress codes, and restrictions on the activities of women. The fundamentalists have a particular disdain for nonpracticing, secularized Muslims. Their ideal is to establish political states where "the true Islam" will be embraced and vigorously enforced through sharia law. Likewise, while many Muslims might hope to convert the whole world to Islam, only the fundamentalists would be willing to do so by coercion. And from there it is only a short step to violence and terrorism.

❀ ❀ ❀

Finally, we will address what is sometimes called "Catholic fundamentalism." As noted earlier, fundamentalism begins as a reaction. In the case of Catholics, the pivotal point was the Second Vatican Council. Very few Catholics were opposed to the calling of the council, mostly because of their high regard for Pope John XXIII and their awareness that past ecumenical councils had been beneficial for the life of the Church. But with the close of the council and the beginning of the changes in parish life, some Catholics were disturbed. They disliked the change from Latin to local languages in the Mass, the rotation of the altar to face the congregation, and the removal of the Communion rail. Some resisted the stress on "active participation" in the Mass, feeling forced to pray and sing with the rest of the congregation. Others lamented what they saw as the poor quality of religious education for their children, especially the discontinuance of exclusive reliance in the United States on *The Baltimore Catechism* for religious education of children and even adults.

These Catholics, like all fundamentalists, felt justified in their criticisms. They pointed to the negative "fallout" from the changes: a spike in the number of priests and nuns leaving the priesthood and the religious life, ill-conceived liturgical "experiments," disregard of Church authority (as exemplified by the widespread rejection of the encyclical on birth control), theologians openly dissenting from Church teachings, clergy and laity refusing obedience to their bishops, the steep decline in new vocations to the priesthood and religious life, and the disregard for previously held norms of sexual morality.

In reaction, these Catholics (both clergy and laity) banded together to try to stem the tide. They formed their own organizations. They wrote to and met with bishops, asking them to intervene and discipline those who appeared to be dissenting from approved teachings and norms. They created new periodicals (and eventually websites and blogs) to publicize their views.

For the most part, this fundamentalist response has been carried out in a relatively thoughtful and dignified manner. Sometimes, however, it has taken the form of diatribe, name-calling, harsh words, and punitive actions. Priests, nuns, lay leaders, and even bishops have received hate mail, threatening phone calls, and other kinds of harassment. Some have even been driven from their assignment. The level of anger and bitterness has at times been astonishing, if not scandalous.

Some Consequences of Fundamentalism

It could be argued that every religion could use a fundamentalist wing. Because the religious sentiment is so powerful a force in human experience, it can easily be distorted. There is a natural tendency, after a burst of religious fervor, for the individual and/or the group to "settle down" into a more monotonous form of expression. That is why reform movements continually emerge in religious institutions. Someone stands up and says, "We have lost our initial inspiration. We have become complacent and listless. We need to return to our roots, our first love." Prophetic voices like these have spurred genuine reform and renewal of many a religious enterprise. This is a positive form of fundamentalism.

> *Problems arise when the reform movement or the personal faith conviction becomes rigid and inflexible.*

On an individual basis, fundamentalism can be "good for the soul." What Protestant, Islamic and Catholic fundamentalism all have in common is a satisfying, personal conviction that "I have found the truth." History is filled with examples of people who have wandered aimlessly and searched anxiously for answers to life's persistent questions, and finally come to inner peace—whether through the Bible or the Qur'an or the Real Presence of Christ in the Eucharist. They have no desire to question or to search further.

Problems arise when the reform movement or the personal faith conviction becomes rigid and inflexible. The human mind is made for truth, but it also seeks deeper understanding, as the medieval scholastic philosophers taught.

Thus, when a Protestant fundamentalist says, "I am saved because I have given my life to Jesus Christ," would we not expect that person to inquire further, "What are the implications of that decision? How do I deepen it, how do I express it in daily life?" When a Muslim fundamentalist says, "Great is Allah," would we not ask, "Can you say what makes Allah great? What are some of his attributes that comfort or challenge you?" When a Catholic fundamentalist says, "I believe it because the Church teaches it," wouldn't it be right to ask, "What is the basis for the Church's teaching?"

Plato is supposed to have said, "The life which is unexamined is not worth living." So it may also be said that "the faith which is unexamined is not worth embracing."

Sometimes it seems that what "drives" fundamentalism is fear. If I allow my beliefs to be challenged or placed under scrutiny, what will happen? Will I lose my sense of serenity, my peace of mind? Will I lose the support of my like-minded friends? If I have to concede that some of my beliefs cannot be fully or rationally explained, can I still hold them as true yet mysterious? Or will I go into a panic and abandon them altogether?

When left unchecked, fundamentalism can breed intolerance. Sister Mary Frances Reis in her article "Fundamentalism on the College Campus" quotes a Catholic student as saying, "I came to Mass today (November 1), though it was the hardest thing I ever did. My roommates kept yelling at me and saying I was going to hell because I came to worship the saints." Another student, a former Catholic turned Protestant fundamentalist, tells her friends, "My mom and dad are going to hell. I tried to save them, but they wouldn't join my church." Fundamentalist attacks on Catholicism are not limited to college campuses. I myself have found pamphlets on my car windshield calling upon Catholics to renounce their "damnable" beliefs and their "devilish" rituals so that they can be saved from the fires of hell.

Islamic fundamentalism often shows its intolerance on a socio-political level. In her book *The Trouble with Islam*, Irshad Manji documents the fierce strain of intolerance among some Muslims:

> Recently, a Shia Ismaili Muslim testified to the U.S. Congress about what happened when the Saudis annexed his hometown of Najran: 'Not only were the Najranis religiously subjugated,' said Ali Alyami, 'but the means of their livelihood were reduced drastically. Most of the fertile farmland was expropriated by the Wahabbi governors, emirs, and judges. In addition, Wahabbis forcefully took half of what Ismailis produced from their farms and animals....'

Manji explains that Saudis regard Shiite Muslims as heretics. Shiites cannot be represented in a Saudi court, and only Wahabbis are appointed as judges. Here religious intolerance has spilled over into political injustice: Shiites in Saudi Arabia have been stripped of their legal rights because their faith conflicts with the ruling fundamentalist group.

Finally, if you read Catholic publications, you are familiar with many sad examples of Catholic fundamentalist intolerance. How often has a small group or sect of Catholics been able to pressure a parish or diocese to "disinvite" a speaker from coming and making a presentation because he or she was unacceptable to the small group? Just one example of this type of censorship involves a well-respected priest I happen to know (for his sake I won't use his name).

This priest was invited to conduct a four-evening mission for a parish. It seemed to be going well until after the second evening when the pastor cancelled the rest of the mission. He told the priest that it was because some of the attendees were disturbed by his emphasis on social justice issues and their implementation (or lack thereof) in the world as well as in the Church. Clearly, Protestants, Islamics and Catholics have their strains of fundamentalism to address.

SACRED BOOKS:
SOURCES OF BELIEF

Jews, Christians and Muslims are often referred to as "People of the Book." That is, they claim that their religious beliefs are not of human origin but are based on revelations received from God and written down in holy books. Jews revere the Hebrew Scriptures (Old Testament); Christians derive their faith from both the Old and New Testaments; and Muslims follow the Qur'an. But in all these religions, there are major differences between fundamentalists and mainline believers in the way these sacred writings are interpreted and manifested in daily life.

Protestant Fundamentalism

As we saw earlier, Martin Luther raised the cry *sola Scriptura* ("the Bible alone") as his central doctrine and rallying point against the Catholic Church of his time. He had become convinced that the Church had departed from the teachings of Scripture in favor of "man-made" doctrines taught by popes and theologians. This, he claimed, had obscured the simple message of the Bible and left the faithful starving for spiritual nourishment. He saw no need for any extrinsic teaching authority to "interpret" the Bible for the faithful; God's word is plain enough to be understood by any sincere believer or seeker.

It is doubtful that Luther foresaw the full consequences of this position: If every believer must interpret the Bible personally, what is to prevent different individuals or groups from forming contradictory interpretations of the text? That is what began to happen even during Luther's lifetime. For example, even though Luther denied that the Mass was a sacrifice, he still believed, in some sense, in the Real Presence of Christ in the Eucharist. But other reformers disagreed. Most important of these was the great Swiss reformer Ulrich Zwingli; and before long everyone was debating the matter of the Eucharist. Eventually Luther and Zwingli had a meeting at Marburg to discuss the issue. They ended the meeting still in disagreement. One historian comments: "The Marburg colloquy was a failure. Theologically, it had confirmed that Protestantism was a divided house. This fact, bitter though it was, gave lie to the exuberant Protestant assertion that men everywhere would agree to the meaning of Scripture if they were only of good will.... The failure to attain agreement meant that both sides clung to their respective theological positions with unwavering determination. The consequences were both far-reaching and disastrous" (Hans J. Hillerbrand, *Christendom Divided*, 1971, p. 127).

One of the "disastrous" consequences was the tendency for the Protestant churches to continue to splinter—so that today there are at least 35,000 different denominations of Protestant Christians, all claiming the Bible as their source of belief. This is why most mainline churches, both Protestant and Catholic, no longer hold to a rigid, Bible-alone theology. They admit the need for some kind of authority structure to clarify and explain the meaning of Scriptural passages.

Fundamentalist Protestants, however, continue to insist on "the Bible alone" as the sole standard of belief—even though, ironically, the expression "Bible alone" appears nowhere in Scripture. They pride themselves on being "Bible-believing" Christians. But since all Christians (as well as Jews) accept the authority of the Scriptures, fundamentalists obviously have something special in mind when they say "Bible-believing." They mean understanding the Bible literally. Doesn't the book of Genesis state that God created the world in six days? Then the scientific evidence for evolution must be dismissed. Does the Bible say the prophet Jonah was swallowed by a great fish and spewed onto the shores of Nineveh? Then that must be literally true, not just a parable. Interestingly, though, these same fundamentalists obviously do not take literally Jesus' words about cutting off one's hand or foot if it becomes an occasion of sin (Matthew 18:8); nor his exhortation to sell all one's possessions and give them to the poor (Matthew 19:21); nor his command to the disciples to wash one another's feet (John 13:14).

So the Bible is not as plain and simple as the fundamentalists would like to believe. As a matter of fact, when they are pressed, they will admit that the Bible needs to be interpreted. Accordingly, their scholars have worked to produce lengthy "commentaries" on the biblical books. One of the most popular is the *Liberty Commentary on the New Testament*, edited by the late Jerry Falwell. Even more influential is the famous *Scofield Reference Bible*, written by C.I. Scofield, and its updated version, *The New Scofield Reference Bible*.

The purpose of the commentaries is to help these Christians understand the true meaning of the Bible. Fundamentalists claim that the devout reader can understand the text with the help of the Holy Spirit. Still, they recognize the danger of every reader interpreting the text in his or her own way, which would result in biblical anarchy. The commentaries do not solve all the problems, however, as they are generally circulated only among pastors and preachers, and the different commentaries often disagree with each other.

What then is the Bible reader to think? Where can he or she turn for an authoritative interpretation of a puzzling passage? Fundamentalists answer, "To the pastor." Though fallible himself, he has been entrusted with God's infallible word. As Jerry Falwell used to put it, the pastor is "God's man," and therefore his directives are to be obeyed by the Christian disciple.

So now we have come full circle. Protestant fundamentalists begin with the claim that the Bible is inspired by God and cannot contain error. It is a plain book that can be understood by plain people who read it with faith. The believer is guided by the Holy Spirit, so there is no need for church authority. Yet believers are not allowed to interpret the text any way they choose. If they do not have access to the approved commentaries, they are to submit their questions and even their views to the authority of the pastor. In his study of a fundamentalist Christian school, Alan Peshkin quotes a student disgruntled with the quality of church music: "The Bible distinctly says, you know, take trumpets and cymbals and stuff and praise the Lord. Over here (in my fundamentalist church), if you don't have just a piano or organ, it's wrong; it's a sin." It is ironic that some Catholics who left the Church because they found it too authoritarian are willing to accept an even more rigid authority structure in a fundamentalist church.

It is ironic that some Catholics who left the Church because they found it too authoritarian are willing to accept an even more rigid authority structure in a fundamentalist church.

It is not difficult to see how insistence on "the Bible alone" can give rise to the two "marks" of fundamentalism that we noted in the first chapter: intolerance and militancy. These Christians are taught that they alone have the truth of the Bible. They memorize a number of biblical texts that they take literally and use them to "convict" others. If the listener disagrees, he or she is told that they are resisting the Spirit of God. For instance, one of their most frequent Bible quotes is from the words of Jesus at the Last Supper: "I am the way, and the truth, and the life. No one comes to the Father except through me" (John 14:6). Fundamentalist Protestants insist that this means only those who profess belief in Jesus Christ will be saved; all others will be damned. Their passionate zeal to convert not only unchurched Christians, but also practicing Jews, Muslims, Buddhists and Catholics—all of whom are presumed to be outside "the true fold"—springs from that central belief. It is this intolerance and militancy that turns away many who might otherwise be drawn to Christianity.

Islamic Fundamentalism

As noted above, the Muslim sacred text is the Qur'an, which is said to have been revealed by God (through the angel Gabriel) to Muhammad over a period of time. Muslim scholars insist that only the original Arabic is the authentic text; translations are not considered genuine revelation. Muhammad was aware of both Jewish and Christian Scriptures and revered them also as God's word. However, he believed they were incomplete, so the texts of the Qur'an constitute the final, definitive revelation of God. Muhammad chose the word Islam for the new religion; the word literally means "submission" or "surrender." He chose the name because he was warning all people to submit entirely to the will of the one, all-powerful God: Allah. As for Muhammad's followers, they would be called Muslims, "those who submit."

The Qur'an is arranged by chapters and verses, but not in chronological order. Rather, it is by length of the chapters, the longest ones being first. Remarkably, the Qur'an accepts that Jesus was born of a virgin (Mary); however, it does not regard him as divine, nor that he was crucified: "Nay, God raised him up" (4:158). Muhammad's most serious problem was with the Christian doctrine of the Trinity, because it goes against the single most important belief of Islam: the oneness of God: "Say not 'Trinity'; desist. It will be better for you. For God is One God" (4:171).

The vast majority of Muslims are not fundamentalists, as we have been using the term. They tend to be moderate or even secularist, desiring to live peacefully alongside non-Muslim neighbors. The fundamentalists, however, would like their whole society to be governed by the teachings of their religion. They believe that the demands of Islamic law are divine, unchanging, and central to the vitality of Islamic society. Only when families are living according to Islamic law can the community be in harmony with God; only when all communities in a nation are living according to Islamic law can the nation be in harmony with God; and only when all nations are living according to Islamic law can the universe be in harmony with God. It is not difficult to see where this worldview can lead. Fundamentalist Muslims dream of one world united by the religion of Islam and living under strict sharia law.

Historically, and up to the present, much of the concern centers around the place of women. In many countries throughout the Muslim world, fundamentalists continue in their efforts to keep women out of the job market, to require them to remain fully veiled in public, and to keep wives in strict submission to their husbands. Such efforts strictly enforce Islamic law in regard to marriage, divorce, inheritance, and succession.

Fundamentalists have achieved varying degrees of success in these matters. Among the most notable instances are Afghanistan's Taliban (now removed from power) and Saudi Arabia's Wahabbi-driven suppression of women. Although repulsive to modern Western societies, the strict control of women is pivotal to Islamic fundamentalists. "Disorderly" women signify a society separated from the will of God. Without doubt the coming years will see repeated clashes between Islamic fundamentalists and the Westernized world concerning the role of women in society.

One other area of tension between Muslim fundamentalists and moderates involves the concept of freedom. Fundamentalists believe that Muslims have been seduced by Western notions of individual self-expression, which clash with the traditional Islamic virtues of obedience and submission to the will of God. In their view, the individual's primary responsibility is to live out "the five pillars" of Islam (to be described in the next chapter) and to work for God's ultimate sovereignty over the entire universe. Freedom must be curtailed because it is opposed to a social order founded upon strict hierarchical structures of obedience.

It must be emphasized that there are multiple forms of Islam practiced throughout the world, just as there are many forms of Christianity and Judaism. Moreover, there are different strands of Islamic fundamentalism, though all are characterized by intolerance and militancy, our two marks of fundamentalism. Some seek to impose strict Islamic law only on fellow Muslims; others are intent on converting non-Muslims to "the true faith." Some would allow only peaceful means of doing so, while others would not hesitate to use violence and terrorism to bring about one worldwide religion: Islam.

Catholic Fundamentalism

Along with all Christians, fundamentalist Catholics revere the Bible as the primary source of their faith. In practice, however, they often appear to give more weight to *The Catechism of the Catholic Church* and to directives and statements from the Vatican. They use these pronouncements to criticize what they perceive as "liberal" ideas and practices in their parishes, dioceses and the Church in general. In turn, their critics label them as "super-Catholics," "reactionaries," and "pre-Vatican II" believers. Unfortunately, this type of polarization has created a great deal of divisiveness within the Church: traditionalists vs. progressives, conservatives vs. liberals, and so on.

It would be wrong to stereotype fundamentalist Catholics as an elderly, uneducated remnant that will soon die out. The fact is, many of them are young, well educated (including theology), and articulate. They write scholarly books, publish their own magazines, have their own list of favorite speakers, and create websites. What they have in common with fundamentalism is their insistence that they alone are proclaiming the truth of the Catholic Church and their intolerance of all other viewpoints.

Fundamentalist Catholics are highly visible in issues related to the liturgy. Some have succeeded in obtaining permission to celebrate the Eucharist in Latin and in the Tridentine rite. But more common is their insistence that the priest and other ministers observe every detail of the approved rites without any deviation or variation. Thus, if the priest omits or changes any of the words or gestures prescribed in the Sacramentary, no matter how minor, he will be confronted. And if he does not conform, he will be reported to the bishop. Even changing the word "men" to "persons" when both genders are obviously intended will be met with a rebuke. Other examples of divergence that can incur criticism include: omitting the washing of the fingers, leaving the altar to exchange the Sign of Peace with the congregation, inviting the people to join hands for the Lord's Prayer, occasionally allowing a woman religious or a lay person to give a witness talk or reflection at the time of the homily, permitting girls to act as altar servers. It matters not that the priest may be an otherwise ideal pastor: He celebrates the Eucharist reverently, preaches in ways that connect the Scriptures with the lives of the people, is available for the sacraments, visits the sick and the homebound, is compassionate for those who are troubled, and reaches out to inactive Catholics and the unchurched. If he deviates in some minor way from the rubrics, he may incur the wrath of what some have called "the liturgical police."

Catholic fundamentalists are also very concerned about

doctrinal orthodoxy. If a parish invites a speaker whom they consider to be too liberal or too feminist, they will raise objections or even pressure the diocese to have the speaker "disinvited." They will check out the books and syllabi of teachers in Catholic schools and colleges to make sure they are orthodox; if not, they will organize to have those resources removed. Pastors' homilies are scrutinized for any sign of deviance from or questioning of Catholic doctrine. If he expresses some degree of compassion for divorced or homosexual persons, for example, he may be denounced.

There is no doubt that some priests and laity have propagated viewpoints and practices that are out of line with authentic Catholicism. Certainly, we need voices in the Church that will challenge and correct the excesses that overly liberal Catholics might fall into, just as we need voices to resist the momentum of overly conservative Catholics. But fundamentalist Catholics often come across as harsh and mean-spirited. They use language like "heretics," "enemies of the Church," and "subversives" to describe those with whom they disagree. They create a climate of fear and suspicion that makes any kind of dialogue difficult.

Because Catholicism embodies such a rich treasury of teaching, it encourages people to think, to ask questions, to discuss and to clarify various points of view. In every period of Church history, such creativity has enriched our understanding of the great mysteries of our faith. It would be tragic if fundamentalism were allowed to squelch this healthy spirit.

"ARE YOU SAVED?"

Nearly every religion takes a stand on the nature of human beings, their purpose and destiny. Humans are the only species we know of that asks questions such as: Where did we come from? What is the purpose of our existence? What happens to us after we die? So it is only natural that fundamentalist Protestants, Muslims and Catholics will have answers to these questions. It may be surprising, however, to see how diverse the answers can be.

Protestant Fundamentalism

If you have ever had a conversation with a Protestant fundamentalist, very likely you have been asked the question, "Are you saved?" This question has a great deal of meaning for fundamentalists, but most other people find it puzzling; they don't know how to answer.

Christians in general share a fairly common understanding of the word "salvation." It means that we, individually and as a species, are in some kind of trouble—what the Bible calls "sin." We are spiritually flawed, inclined to self-indulgence and all other forms of evil, and alienated from friendship with God. Therefore we need help, we need to be "saved" from this unhappy state. The good news: in Jesus Christ, God has forgiven our sins, reconciled with us in a bond of friendship and love, and given us a firm hope for eternal life in the world to come. This salvation is not our own achievement; it was won for us through the death and resurrection of Jesus Christ.

So far so good. The question remains, however: What is our part in salvation? The Bible is clear that God wants all people to be saved (1 Timothy 2:4). At the same time, God will not force salvation on us. God respects our free will, so we have the awesome capacity to either accept or reject salvation.

The question then becomes: How do we take hold of the

salvation Christ won for us? The fundamentalists would say that happens when we make a personal decision to accept Jesus Christ as our Lord and Savior: "Confess your sins and receive Jesus into your heart." In other words, in a moment of truth and grace, I come to the realization that I am on a downward spiritual path. Feeling the guilt and weight of my own sins and feeling my utter powerlessness to turn my life around by my own efforts, I come to believe that Jesus Christ gave his life for me on the cross and thereby "paid the price" for my sins once and for all. I don't have to keep trying so hard to be perfect; all I have to do is commit my life to Christ and let him be my Savior. This is what it means to be "born again."

A number of consequences flow from this theology of salvation. Note, first of all, that "the saving act" is a purely internal one. There is no need for any external ritual or public ceremony. Some fundamentalists do not even believe in the necessity of baptism, except as an external sign of the great event that has taken place internally. And nearly all fundamentalists reject infant baptism. They see it as a meaningless ritual, since the baby is incapable of making a conscious commitment to Christ.

Second, fundamentalist Protestants believe that once they have made this decisive commitment, their salvation is absolutely assured. This is why they exude such spiritual self-confidence and why they can't understand it when Catholics seem to "waffle" about their salvation: "Well, gee, I hope I'll be saved, but I suppose I can blow it if I'm not careful." Fundamentalists don't understand such talk. For them, once you accept Christ into your heart, he will never abandon you. Not even if you go back to a life of sin? No—your sins cannot invalidate your salvation. The only way you can be lost is to explicitly repudiate your act of commitment to Christ. The slogan is, "Once saved, always saved."

I once asked a fundamentalist pastor about this: "Do you

mean to say that if I give myself to Christ, but then live like a pagan, disregard the commandments of God, and so on—I will still be saved in the end?" He answered by making a distinction between "salvation" and "retribution." Yes, salvation is once-for-all, because God is faithful to his promise. But I will certainly experience retribution: God will send me setbacks, failures, sickness, and so on, in an effort to bring me back to my senses. But no—I will not be lost unless I formally reject Jesus Christ.

This is certainly a comforting doctrine, but it strains credibility. Is suffering and sickness always a sign of divine retribution? The whole purpose of the book of Job is to correct that wrong idea. And all of us know people who, like Job, are models of innocence and upright living, yet they suffer in innumerable ways. Conversely, the world is full of drug dealers, con-artists, violent predators, and others who live like kings and queens with no evidence of divine retribution. And some of them claim to be born-again Christians. One has to wonder if this kind of theology contributed to the downfall of some of the televangelists.

A third consequence of the fundamentalist view of salvation is a narrow, exclusionary idea of who can or will be saved. For one thing, salvation is limited to those who accept Christ as their Savior. This automatically excludes Jews, Muslims, and members of all non-Christian religions. Moreover, it is limited to Christians who have been "born again," who have surrendered their lives to Christ in the specific manner described above. Everyone else is literally on the road to hell. This is what accounts for the evangelistic fervor of Protestant fundamentalists. They sincerely believe it is their mission to persuade as many people as possible to make a soul-saving decision for Christ. It also explains the negative side: their intolerance, sometimes bordering on fanaticism, for those who do not believe as they do.

Islamic Fundamentalism

For all Muslims, salvation (entering heaven or paradise) is the fruit of submission (obedience) to the will of God. The will of God is expressed in the five tenets or "pillars" of Islam:

Recitation of the creed

"There is no god but Allah, and Muhammad is the prophet of Allah."

Prayer five times a day

These are said just before dawn; at noon; mid-afternoon; just after sunset; and at bedtime. The Friday noon prayer usually takes place at a mosque, where the faithful gather to pray together to reinforce the spirit of the Muslim community. Men and women pray separately in the mosque, with the women's section off to one side or on a balcony. The Qur'an does not oblige women to pray five times if their household or motherly duties interfere, and women are encouraged to pray at home rather than at the mosque on Fridays. The Friday prayer also includes a teaching session conducted by the community's leader, the imam, and a larger meeting for the surrounding community is held at least twice a year.

Almsgiving

Charity is not merely encouraged but is a religious obligation and a mark of devotion to God. It is intended to help the poor, to purify oneself, and to provide a means to salvation.

Fasting

During the entire month of Ramadan, Muslims are to refrain from eating, drinking, smoking, and sexual intercourse from daybreak till sunset. Ramadan commemorates the month when the angel Gabriel dictated the Qur'an to Muhammad. The fast is intended to strengthen self-control.

The hajj (pilgrimage) to Mecca in Saudi Arabia

The hajj has been called "the zenith of a Muslim's life." Those who are physically fit and financially able should make the hajj at least once before they die. It is truly a once-in-a-lifetime experience, an extraordinary display of equality and brotherhood. Muslims from the Middle East, from Asia, Africa, Europe, and the Americas wear similar white garments and perform the same rituals and ceremonies without regard to their wealth, nationality, or social position. For many, the pilgrimage brings a sense of joy in belonging to a worldwide community.

Many Muslims also feel bound to a sixth pillar: *jihad*. The word literally means "struggle," and appears often in the Qur'an. Moderate Muslims say it refers to the individual's or the community's duty to "strive in the way of God"—the constant but peaceful struggle to live virtuously, to do good, and to avoid bad habits. Many say this was the original meaning of the concept in the Qur'an.

For fundamentalist Muslims, however, jihad has come to mean "holy war" in the context of the Qur'an's commands to fight against infidels, or "disbelievers." Many believe that Islam is in a state of permanent jihad aimed at converting the whole world, but not necessarily by force. The Saudi government's translation of the Qur'an says in its notes that jihad is clearly one of the pillars of Islam:

Al-Jihad (holy fighting) in Allah's Cause (with full force of numbers and weaponry) is given the utmost importance in Islam and is one of its pillars (on which it stands). By Jihad, Islam is established. Allah's Word is made superior.... By abandoning Jihad (may Allah protect us from that) Islam is destroyed and the Muslims fall into an inferior position; their honor is lost, their lands are stolen, their rule and authority vanish. Jihad is an obligatory duty in Islam on every Muslim. (Ed Hotaling, *Islam Without Ilustions*, p. 76)

While most Muslims would probably reject this kind of language, fundamentalists would embrace it. But who has the authority to declare a jihad? Officially, only the government; but in practice the real answer seems to be anyone who can get away with it, such as Osama bin Laden. Also, despite the belief that Islam is one brotherhood, jihad has often been invoked to justify Muslims fighting against one another.

Catholic Fundamentalism

Like Catholics in general, fundamentalist Catholics accept the view of salvation taught by the Church. This will be laid out more fully in the next chapter. Briefly, salvation begins with baptism, is deepened and furthered by participation in the other sacraments and by obedience to the commandments, and culminates with the gift of eternal life with God in heaven.

Catholic fundamentalists put a great deal of emphasis on holding correct beliefs, as taught by the hierarchy and summarized in *The Catechism of the Catholic Church*. Fundamentalist parents tend to be extremely involved in their childrens' Catholic schools and religious education programs, and they are often overly critical of the teachers, their methods, and teaching resources. When it comes to higher education, these fundamentalist Catholics are often disheartened with Catholic colleges and universities; they perceive these schools as being too secular in their outlook and watering down or even opposing traditional Catholic beliefs and practices. In response to this, many fundamentalist Catholic parents have begun sending their children to one of a number of recently founded colleges and universities that expressly uphold Catholic theology and spiritual values.

Fundamentalist Catholics are usually highly visible in the pro-life movement. They turn out in large numbers for pro-life marches and rallies. They pray and picket at abortion clinics and sometimes try to talk women out of going through with an abortion. They provide help for women who are needy but choose to have their baby. They lend their support to candidates for public office who hold to pro-life positions and work to defeat those who are pro-choice. Also, in line with Church teaching, they are likely to teach and practice natural family planning as an alternative to artificial contraception.

Besides their faithful attendance at Sunday and holyday Masses, these Catholics often engage in devotional practices as aids to salvation. The rosary is a favorite prayer for many, as well as the Divine Mercy chaplet. Some try to spend an hour or more each week in adoration of Christ in the Blessed Sacrament. The lives of the Virgin Mary and the saints have a strong appeal for these Catholics; they provide inspiration to live their faith generously in a secularized world. This interest in Mary and the

> *The passion for orthodoxy can sometimes trump basic charity and decency.*

saints has produced an abundance of new books, videos, and DVD's that are readily available, especially through a number of Catholic websites on the Internet. And speaking of media, it has been mostly traditional Catholics who have founded new Catholic radio networks as well as the only 24-hour television station EWTN.

In fairness, it must be said that not all Catholics who regard themselves as "conservative" or "traditional" are fundamentalists in the sense that we defined earlier. Recall the two special characteristics of fundamentalism: intolerance and militancy. Many conservative and traditionalist Catholics, while they may be strong in their viewpoints, do not demonstrate those qualities.

At the same time, we must acknowledge the darker side of Catholic fundamentalism. The passion for orthodoxy can sometimes trump basic charity and decency. It is sad to see good teachers or parish staff members lose their jobs because of the pressure of a small group of conservative parishioners. Often the cases could have been resolved fairly and peacefully if the parties had been willing to dialogue in a true Christian spirit. Fundamentalist Catholics can be angry and mean-spirited in their criticism of their "adversaries." The conviction that "we alone possess the truth" can undercut any attempt to reach an understanding or mutually agreeable compromise.

Moreover, forbidding our young people to question their beliefs does not prepare them well to meet the objections and attacks on their faith that will inevitably come when they encounter the wider world. There is no need for the "deconstruction" that sometimes goes on in liberal Scripture and theology classes. But students must be informed about the honest questions that scholars and scientists raise about matters of faith and be equipped to respond intelligently. Finally, fundamentalist Catholics must remember that theirs is not the only way to salvation. It is distressing to see people trying to impose their personal devotions and religious practices on others: "How can you call yourself a Catholic if you don't follow this or that?" The truth is that one of the great blessings of being Catholic is that, within the framework of creed-sacraments-commandments, there are many paths to salvation as well as to holiness.

CATHOLIC RESPONSES TO FUNDAMENTALISM

As noted in the Introduction, this book is written primarily for Catholics and secondarily for anyone who wishes to better understand Catholic teachings. The present chapter will attempt to explain the Catholic viewpoint on the main tenets of fundamentalism. We will focus mainly on Protestant fundamentalism, since that is what most Catholics are likely to encounter.

I. Catholics and the Bible

It is no secret that Catholics generally are not very knowledgeable about the Bible. So they often feel intimidated when their Protestant friends quote biblical passages that seem to contradict Catholic beliefs or practices. Thankfully, this has begun to change as more Catholics are being encouraged to read the Bible and participate in Bible study courses. But this would be a good place to outline some basic principles for understanding the Bible.

In the first place, Catholics agree with fundamentalists that the Bible is the inspired word of God. The Second Vatican Council states that all the books of the Old and New Testaments are sacred because they "have been written down under the inspiration of the Holy Spirit and ... they have God as their author" (*Dogmatic Constitution on Divine Revelation*, n. 11).

Nevertheless, we must not think of God as "author" in the sense that God "dictated" the whole Bible word for word. Rather, as the Council says, God chose human writers and "made use of their powers and abilities so that with (God) acting in them and through them they, as true authors, consigned to writing all those things and only those things which (God) wanted" (ibid.).

The Church takes this notion of human authorship very

seriously. The Council goes on to encourage biblical scholars to study the historical and cultural circumstances in which the various books were composed—as well as their literary form—in order to understand them better. It also states that any biblical passage must not be taken in isolation or out of context, but must be read and interpreted in light of the Bible as a whole.

> *The Catholic Church also teaches that the Bible is without error, but with this important difference: inerrancy extends only to the religious truths of the Bible, those which are necessary or important for our spiritual life and eternal salvation.*

As long ago as 1943, Pope Pius XII encouraged Catholic biblical scholars to study the sacred texts in their original languages (Hebrew and Greek) and within the context of their cultural and literary expressions. The Church, he said, has nothing to fear from this kind of scientific study of the Bible; on the contrary, it can vastly enrich our understanding of God's word. Fundamentalists, on the other hand, reject this approach to the Bible as a dangerous kind of "modernism" that will undermine the faith of Christians.

This leads us to the question of biblical *inerrancy*, a point on which fundamentalists and Catholics differ. Fundamentalists insist that the Bible is absolutely free of error. If it states that God formed Adam out of the clay of the earth and Eve out of Adam's rib, it must be so. If it says that the sun stood still in the sky for a whole day or that Jonah was in the fish's belly for three days, it must be so. For if the Bible is "wrong" on any matter, how can we be sure it is true about anything, including the death and resurrection of Christ?

The Catholic Church also teaches that the Bible is without error, but with this important difference: inerrancy extends only to the *religious* truths of the Bible, those which are necessary or important for our spiritual life and eternal salvation. There may well be scientific or historical errors in the Bible, as well as literary exaggerations; but these in no way diminish our faith in the Bible as the source of religious truth. The sacred writers were simply not interested in teaching science, history or psychology. They accepted the common views of their time and culture, and God guided them in their task of recording God's wonderful deeds and teaching God's wise ways for the spiritual good of the human race.

So, for example, Catholics would find no contradiction between the creation accounts in Genesis and the gradual formation of the universe over billions of years. Genesis is simply teaching the profound religious truth that God is the ultimate Source and Creator of all that exists, that God guided in a wondrous manner the forces that shaped our universe and allowed for the evolution of the species.

Likewise, it is no threat to our faith when contemporary Scripture scholars say that the Book of Jonah is most likely not a "true" historical account; rather, it is a parable (much like the Good Samaritan story in the Gospel) that teaches a beautiful religious truth: God's willingness to forgive even pagan peoples who repent.

The major point Catholics make is this: the Bible is not always a "plain" book, any more than Shakespeare's plays are "plain." The ordinary reader can always find inspiration and guidance from reading the Bible prayerfully, just as he or she can gain insight into human nature by reading Shakespeare. But because the Bible can too easily be misunderstood, it needs (at least sometimes) to be clarified and interpreted.

It is interesting that this need for help in interpretation is expressed in the Bible itself. When the Ethiopian official was reading the words of the prophet Isaiah, Philip the deacon asked him, "Do you understand what you are reading?" The man replied, "How can I, unless someone guides me?" (Acts 8:30-31). Similarly, Catholics have always felt the need for some guidance in reading the Scriptures because of the all-too-human tendency to misinterpret and misunderstand. One of the letters of Peter also warns about this tendency. Speaking of St. Paul's letters he says, "There are some things in them hard to understand, which the ignorant and unstable twist to their own destruction, as they do the other scriptures" (2 Peter 3:16).

The Place of Tradition

How then do Catholics hope to avoid the pitfalls of misunderstanding or distorting the meaning of the Bible? For one thing, like fundamentalists, we depend on the guidance of the Holy Spirit, which we seek in prayer. We believe that God truly does speak to us, enlighten us, comfort us, and challenge us when we read the Bible prayerfully. At the same time, we take care not to isolate the Bible from the ongoing life of the Church or from our spiritual life as a whole. Our reading of the Bible is not strictly a private matter; we want to do it in the context of the Christian community. That is what Catholics mean by "Tradition."

Tradition is simply the set of beliefs held by the Christian community and handed down by word of mouth from one generation to the next. An important truth often forgotten by both Catholics and fundamentalist Protestants is that the community we call "the Church" was in existence long before the book we know as "the Bible" came into being. As someone once put it, "It was the Church that gave us the Bible, not the other way around."

Which leads to an interesting question: How, then, was the Bible formed? First, it is crucial to remember that we learn who God is mainly through the stories of God's *actions* throughout history: creation, the call of Abraham, the Exodus, the covenant between God and the Jews, the exile in Baby-lon and the return of God's people to the land of Israel. Long before these events were written down, people remembered these wonderful deeds of God and recounted them for their children. Eventually, various authors wrote them down, under divine inspiration, so that the essential events would not be distorted by the lens of oral tradition.

The same basic pattern followed for the New Testament writings. The stories about the life and teachings of Jesus were handed on by word of mouth. People in those days were used to remembering and recounting stories accurately, since there were no "books" as such, only scrolls that were not readily available. In fact, there was no written "Gospel" until at least three decades after the resurrection of Jesus. Luke, who wrote his Gospel around 80-85 AD, clearly states in his prologue that his material was "handed on" to him by "eyewitnesses and servants of the word" (Luke 1:2). By this time, the letters of Paul, John and Peter were also being circulated among the Christians.

The problem was that many other writings were being put forward and claiming to be authentic stories and sayings of Jesus—the so-called "Gnostic" gospels made famous by the novel *The Da Vinci Code.* These accounts were quite popu-lar in their time and were regarded by some Christians as in-spired. So eventually the question had to be addressed: Which of these writings are inspired (and therefore Scripture), and which are not? Remember, there was no "Bible" as yet. It had not even been decided which of the Old Testament writings were believed to be inspired.

Who has the authority to decide such important matters? History gives us the answer: It was the *community*, especial-ly the elders (presbyters and bishops), who would gather in councils to prayerfully discern which writings were in harmony with the oral tradition that had been handed on from generation to generation. Both Protestants and Catholics believe that the Church community was guided by the Holy Spirit in these decisions. It was not until almost the end of the fourth century that Church councils gave final approval to the present books of the Bible. In his usual blunt manner, St. Augustine once made this statement: "I would put no faith in the Gospels unless the authority of the Catholic Church directed me to do so."

"Canon" of the Bible

Many Catholics go through life never realizing that their Bible contains seven more books than the Protestant Bible. Why is this, and how did it come about? The question has an interesting history. The Old Testament "books" of the Bible were originally written in Hebrew. But in the century or two before Christ, a group of Jewish scholars in Alexandria, Egypt, began working on a translation of the Hebrew Scriptures into Greek. This translation came to be known as "the Septuagint." It soon became very popular, because Greek was becoming the common language of the Mediterranean world and Hebrew was a dying language (Palestinian Jews usually spoke Aramaic, a Hebrew dialect). The Septuagint version contained seven books that were not included in the Palestinian Hebrew version: Wisdom, Sirach, Judith, Tobit, Baruch, and 1 and 2 Maccabees. Both translations were used in the various synagogues where Jews worshipped.

The year 70 AD was a disastrous time for the Jewish community. The Romans reacted to an uprising by destroying the holy city of Jerusalem, including the Temple. The people were stunned and demoralized. Some time later a group of rabbis and other scholars held meetings in the city of Jamnia in order to rally the community and find ways to preserve their ancestral religion. One of the tasks was to decide which of the Jewish sacred books were to be included in the official "canon" of the scriptures. There was general agreement about most of the books, but the canon was not finally fixed until near the end of the second century. The decision was to accept only the Hebrew scriptures and to exclude the extra seven books of the Septuagint.

Meanwhile, similar discussions were taking place among the early Christians.

There was a strong preference for the Greek Septuagint version, since the vast majority (over ninety percent) of the quotations from the Old Testament found in the New Testament were from the Septuagint. So the seven additional books were included in the Christian listing.

When it came to the New Testament, as we have seen, there was also much debate over which books should be included or excluded. Some Christian leaders thought that certain books (Hebrews, Jude, 2 Peter, Revelation) were not inspired, while others held that writings like The Shepherd of Hermas, the Gospels of Peter and Thomas, the letters of Barnabas and Clement, were inspired. It was not until the late fourth century that the canon of Scripture was finally settled. After the Council of Rome in 382, Pope Damasus wrote a decree listing the canon as our present seventy-three books: forty-six of the Old Testament and twenty-seven of the New. Debate continued, however. Then in 397 the Council of Carthage approved the same list of books; and this is the council which even many Protestants regard as the authority for the New Testament books. And in 405, Pope Innocent I again approved the seventy-three-book listing and formally closed the canon of the Bible.

This is how matters remained for the next 1100 years, until the Reformation. In 1529 Martin Luther decided to adopt the thirty-nine-book Hebrew version of the Old Testament. He justified his decision to omit the seven books by appealing to St. Jerome who, around the year 400, had expressed concerns that these Greek texts had no Hebrew counterparts. (It turns out that Jerome was misinformed. Biblical scholars now assure us that there were Hebrew versions of most of these books even in pre-Christian times.) But Luther's real reason appears to have been that some of the books teach doctrines that he rejected: 2 Maccabees encourages prayers for the dead (implying some kind of Purgatory); and Sirach is strong on the importance of "good works" for salvation. In any case, from Luther's time on, Protestant Bibles omit those seven books of the Old Testament. They are named "deutero-canonical" or "apocryphal" to distinguish them from the "canonical" books, and are sometimes included as an appendix.

One might wonder how fundamentalist Protestants reconcile their belief in the Bible as the sole guide (*sola Scriptura*) for faith and salvation, and the 300-plus years before there was a definitive Bible. At any rate, Catholics hold that since the Bible grew out of the believing community under the inspiration of the Holy Spirit, it must be read and interpreted with the help of the community. We have already seen that fundamentalists also rely on the community to help them understand the Bible; they make use of commentaries or consult their pastors. Catholics do the same, the difference being that they have the benefit of 2000 years of the Church community's study, reflection and scholarship, as well as the authoritative teachings of popes and councils. Indeed, the Bible cannot be separated from tradition or from the teaching authority of the popes and bishops. In the early Church, as we have seen, all three "grew up" together.

Muslims and the Qur'an

As noted earlier, Islam's holy book is the Qur'an. Some Christians who have read this holy book find beauty and inspiration in it, while others find it boring and confusing. Muslims say that no translation can do it justice and that it must be read in the original Arabic. It is not always easy to understand, and sometimes there are apparent contradictions. We noted above that the text denies the doctrine of the Trinity as well as the divinity of Christ. However, the Qur'an speaks highly of Jesus as God's prophet and of Mary as a holy virgin.

We will limit ourselves here to a few sections in the Qur'an that Muslim fundamentalists use to justify their thinking and behavior. For instance, one of the "war suras" (chapters) quotes Allah: "I will instill terror into the hearts of the Unbelievers. Smite ye above the necks, and smite all their finger-tips off them" (8:12). And later: "...fight and slay the Pagans wherever ye find them; and seize them, beleaguer them, and lie in wait for them in every stratagem (of war)" (9:5). At another point Muhammad states God's policy since Noah and the great flood: namely, to destroy those who are wicked even though they are given "the good things of this life." First God sends a messenger to warn them—Moses, Jesus or Muhammad himself—but if that is to no avail, he visits them with his wrath:

> When We decide to destroy a population, We first
>   send a definite order
> To those among them who are given the good things
>   of this life, and yet transgress;
> So that the word is proved true against them:
> Then it is: We destroy them utterly.
> How many generations have We destroyed after
>   Noah? (17:16-17).

It is not difficult to see how a Muslim terrorist could read verses like these and twist them to justify violence. On the other hand, most Muslims would understand these and other war suras as calls to work peacefully for the conversion of unbelievers, or perhaps they might view them in a spiritual sense, much as modern Jews and Christians do when reading Old Testament passages where God commands fighting against enemies. Fundamentalist Muslims themselves tend to ignore the fact that the Qur'an initiated a long tradition of compassion and freedom of religion for captured peoples: "Let there be no compulsion in religion" (2:256).

Another theme in the Qur'an that fundamentalists may fixate on is that of martyrdom and the promise of Paradise for those who fight in the cause of Allah. One of the leaders of the 2001 attack on the World Trade Center actually provided his men with a vision of the pleasures of Paradise, in case they forgot. In a house used by Al-Qaeda in Kabul, Afghanistan, U.S. troops found a letter from a militant using the name Abu Yasser. It stressed that "hitting the Americans and Jews is a target of great value and has its rewards in this life and, God willing, in the afterlife." These are just a couple examples of how fundamentalist Islamic terrorists think the Qur'an promises Paradise as a reward for murder.

Sadly, any individual or sect can make use of sacred texts to justify almost any form of irrational, cruel or violent activity. Only God knows how many senseless wars, genocides, purges and persecutions have been perpetrated in the name of religion. All of us stand in need of repentance for these horrors of history.

II. Catholics and Salvation

If Protestant fundamentalists view salvation as a personal decision to accept Jesus Christ as their Lord and Savior, how do Catholics view Salvation?

As we have seen, they agree with fundamentalists that salvation is not a human achievement but is God's work. Nevertheless, Catholics believe it is not a once-and-for-all event; rather, salvation is an ongoing process. In addition, it is not only a private, interior experience of turning to the Lord, but it also includes the public, external rite of baptism.

Based on the Gospel of John, Catholics take baptism very seriously. Early in the text, a Pharisee named Nicodemus comes to talk with Jesus, and Jesus tells him solemnly, "Very truly I tell you, no one can see the kingdom of God without being born from above" (John 3:3). The Greek word *anothen* can mean either "born again" or "born from above," and many versions use the second translation. For our purposes it doesn't matter. But while fundamentalists make use of this verse to justify their insistence on an internal, "born again" experience, it is curious that they ignore what Jesus says only two verses later: "...no one can enter the kingdom of God without being born of water and Spirit" (3:5).

It is clear from history that the early Church interpreted that text as referring to baptism, especially when reading it in the light of Jesus' final words when he commissioned the apostles: "Go, therefore, and make disciples of all nations, baptizing them in the name of the Father and of the Son and of the Holy Spirit" (Matthew 28:19). Moreover, the Acts of the Apostles and the letters of Paul and Peter are filled with references to the importance of baptism for salvation, such as Acts 2:28 and 10:44-48. It is certainly true that baptism without an internal conversion to Christ would be useless for salvation. But it seems equally clear from the Scriptures that, ordinarily, baptism must accompany the interior conversion.

One question yet remains: Why do Catholics put so much stress on the baptism of infants? Babies cannot possibly make a conscious decision to accept Christ as their Savior. Here is an example of Catholics relying on tradition as well as on Scripture for guidance. There are a couple of instances in the Bible in which whole families received baptism, presumably including their young children (see Acts 16:15,33; and 1 Corinthians 1:16). And we know that Christians began the practice of baptizing children and infants in the first centuries after Christ. They believed that baptism joined them to Christ in a profound and radical way and filled them with the gifts of the Holy Spirit. Why should that wonderful grace be denied to children? Besides, infant baptism was a powerful way to proclaim the truth (so firmly held by fundamentalists) that we do not earn our salvation; it is purely God's gift. For here is this little child, having "accomplished" nothing as yet, but being told by God, "You are my child, my beloved, with whom I am well pleased" (see Mark 1:11).

Catholics are aware, however, that baptism is only the beginning of salvation. They agree with fundamentalists that at some point in our adult life, we must make a conscious commitment to Jesus Christ. The mere ritual of baptism will not save us unless we internalize its meaning: "I belong to Christ. I want to live for him, not for myself."

In his fine little book *The Born-Again Catholic*, Albert Boudreau says that what we need to do is place Jesus at the center of our lives, not just leave him at the margin or as "one of many" concerns we may have. Many Catholics have told me that this is exactly what they experienced on a retreat, Marriage Encounter or Cursillo, parish mission, or in the silence of their own hearts. In fact, most mature Catholics say they need to commit themselves to Christ over and over again. This is not to say that they question whether or not they are saved, but rather that they accept the human condition and know that they are weak, forgetful, or influenced by the un-Christian attitudes and values of the society around them.

To speak of salvation as an ongoing process rather than a single event implies something else: Christians have to keep struggling to overcome the forces of sin in themselves and in society and bring more and more of their daily choices into harmony with their commitment to Christ.

Fundamentalists tend to dismiss this notion of salvation as an ongoing process by calling it "saved by good works *instead* of by faith." But Catholics do not claim that they are saved by their own works; they know very well that only the death and resurrection of Jesus has the power to save them. Yet they see in the Bible a very clear connection between *belonging* to Jesus Christ and acting in accord with his teachings. Several passages promote this idea, including the following:

- When Jesus was speaking with his disciples on the night before he died, he told them, "If you love me, you will keep my commandments" (John 14:15). Such obedience is a natural, behavioral consequence of our love for Christ.

- In his Sermon on the Mount, Jesus cautioned his listeners: "Not everyone who says to me 'Lord, Lord' will enter the kingdom of heaven, but only the one who does the will of my Father in heaven" (Matthew 7:21). Clearly, entrance into heaven is contingent upon fulfilling the will of God as well as on belief in Jesus.

- Jesus was very clear when talking about the last judgment that our salvation will depend on how we have responded to the needs of our brothers and sisters, for it is really he whom we serve (see Matthew 25:31-46).

- The Letter of James is crystal clear in stating that both faith in Christ and the practice of good works are necessary for salvation: "What good is it, my brothers and sisters, if you say you have faith but do not have works? Can faith save you? If a brother or sister is naked and lacks daily food, and one of you says to them, 'Go in peace; keep warm and eat your fill,' and yet do not supply their bodily needs, what is the good of that? So faith by itself, if it has no works, is dead" (2:14-17).

In a word, "good works" of themselves do not save us; but if we persist in disobedience to the Lord's commandments, we can forfeit our salvation.

In the matter of salvation, there is another major difference between Catholics and fundamentalist Protestants. Whereas the latter believe they are saved by faith in Jesus Christ and are nourished by the word of God in the Bible, Catholics also believe that they encounter Christ and are nourished by participating in sacred actions called "sacraments." Mainline Protestants generally profess belief in only two sacraments: baptism and confirmation; some also celebrate the Eucharist, but only as a memorial or symbol, not as the real presence of Christ. And fundamentalists regard the notion of sacraments as superstitious rituals, another indication that Catholics put their faith in their own "works" rather than in the saving death of Christ on the cross.

Catholics reply that they do believe in the adequacy of Christ's death for our salvation, but they also believe that his saving actions, flowing from his death on the cross, are made visible and present to us in seven special signs: baptism, confirmation, reconciliation, Eucharist, anointing of the sick, matrimony, and Holy Orders. One of the earliest heresies the Church had to confront was the notion that the visible, material world was evil. Manichaeans, Gnostics, and other groups held to a dualistic view of reality borrowed from Greek philosophy: spirit was good, matter was evil. Against this notion the early Church theologians insisted that the material world, the world of nature, came from the creative hand of God and was therefore good. Indeed, the visible creation can reveal the invisible presence of God. The Psalms of the Bible are filled with poetic expressions of this truth: "The heavens are telling the glory of God, and the firmament proclaims his handiwork" (Psalms 19:1). According to St. Paul, even people without faith are capable of knowing something of God by reflecting on the beauty, order and harmony of the visible creation (see Romans 1:19-20).

Contemporary theologians call this "the sacramental principle"; that is, the visible, material world reveals the presence of invisible, spiritual realities. Ordinarily, we humans do not have direct access to these realities. The exception would be the mystics, who sometimes have a direct experience of God, Jesus, Mary, angels, and the like. But ordinarily, because we ourselves are both body and spirit, we need to see, hear and touch material reality in order to know the spiritual.

This is why the Incarnation of the Son of God is such a key mystery for Christians. By entering our world in human form, Jesus reveals God to us. If we want to know what God is like, we need only contemplate the words and actions of Jesus. When one of his disciples begged him to "show us the Father and we will be satisfied," Jesus answered, "Have I been with you all this time, Philip, and you still do not know me? Whoever has seen me has seen the Father" (John 14:8-9). So, as theologians like to say, Jesus himself is "the original sacrament," the holy presence of God embodied before our eyes. As we say in the Preface of the Mass for Christmas, "In him we see our God made visible, and so are caught up in the love of the God we cannot see."

> *According to St. Paul, even people without faith are capable of knowing something of God by reflecting on the beauty, order and harmony of the visible creation.*

The other application of the sacramental principle involves the sacraments themselves. One good way to understand sacraments is to view them as actions; the actions of Christ extended in space and time. During his days on earth, Jesus forgave sins, healed the sick, changed bread and wine into his body and blood for our spiritual nourishment, and commissioned the apostles to do the same in his memory. Over time, the Church reflected on these actions and concluded that

Jesus had left behind seven special actions or signs wherein the faithful could encounter the risen Christ and receive spiritual help for their pilgrimage on earth. As St. Augustine put it in one of his memorable homilies: When the Church baptizes, it is Christ who baptizes—and likewise confirms, forgives sins, becomes present in the Eucharist, anoints for healing, joins a couple together in sacred marriage, and ordains ministers for service in the Church. There was never a doubt that Christ also meets us through his word in Scripture and in the person of our brothers and sisters. But the sacraments are seen as privileged moments when we are touched by Christ with special graces for times of need in our spiritual journey.

In the light of this theology, we can appreciate the meaning of each sacrament as a special encounter with Christ at key moments in our life:

Baptism

Whether as an infant or an adult, baptism confers a whole new identity upon the person. Just as at the baptism of Jesus, God the Father looks with profound love upon us and says, "You are my beloved son/daughter; in you I am well pleased." This is the "born-again" experience in Catholic theology.

Confirmation

When the Holy Spirit was poured out upon the disciples at Pentecost, they were transformed from confused, fearful people into persons of deep conviction and courage. They were empowered not only to live their faith in Jesus but also to profess it openly and share it with others. In a world that is not always supportive of Christian values, we need the power of the Holy Spirit to strengthen us to live our faith and to share it with others.

Reconciliation

Both the Gospels of John (20:23) and Luke (24:46-49) show Jesus conferring on the apostles the power to forgive sins in his name. Jesus knew that, despite our faith in him, we would sometimes commit sin and then need assurance of his forgiveness. The human need to confess to another human being is deep in our nature—which is why people will "confess" to therapists, bartenders, hairdressers and friends. But none of these can assure them of God's forgiveness. That is the beauty of the sacrament of Reconciliation. The priest forgives our sins, not in his own name, but in the name of Jesus Christ. And he is bound by "the seal of confession" never to reveal the identity of the one who has confessed.

Eucharist

Based on the Gospels and the words of St. Paul (1 Corinthians 11:23-27), Catholics believe that in the ritual of the Mass, the simple elements of bread and wine are transformed into the true body and blood of Jesus Christ. They rejoice in knowing that they are not alone on their earthly pilgrimage: Jesus comes to them in this humble way to be food and drink, spiritual strength for the journey of life. The Eucharist enables them to remain united to Christ, "abide" in him, as he promised: "Those who eat my flesh and drink my blood abide in me and I in them" (John 6:56).

Anointing of the Sick

Everyone gets sick at times, and the Gospels show that Jesus spent much of his time healing sick and troubled people. In this sacrament, the priest's action of anointing with oil and offering prayer is the visible sign that Christ's invisible love and healing power are now being directed to the sick person. The biblical basis for this sacrament comes from the Letter of James: "Are there any among you sick? They should call for the elders of the Church and have them pray over them,

anointing them with oil in the name of the Lord" (5:14). The
intention is that the person will be healed; but if this is not
granted, the prayer asks for strength to bear the burdens of
illness with faith and hope.

Matrimony

Like many religious people, Catholics regard marriage as more
than a civil or secular event. In the Old Testament it was seen
as a symbol of God's love for the people of Israel, a sign of the
covenant between them (Hosea 2:14-20). In the New Testament, St. Paul views marriage between Christians as a sacrament or "mystery" of the love between Christ and his body,
the Church (Ephesians 5:21-33). For these reasons, Catholics
consider marriage to be one of the seven sacraments. As such,
it calls the couple to mutual fidelity and self-sacrificing love,
just as Christ's love is enduring and sacrificial; and it confers
on them the special graces they need to live up to that profound biblical vision.

Holy Orders

How would the saving mission of Jesus continue after his as-
cension into heaven? The first Christians believed that Jesus
had entrusted this mission first of all to the twelve apostles.
Like any community, the Church would need leaders. But as
time went on, the apostles delegated others to take leadership
roles. These came to be known as "overseers" (later, "bishops"), "presbyters" (later, "priests"), and deacons. As primary
leader, the bishop would select and "ordain" presbyters to be
the leaders of local churches and deacons to assist. Holy Orders
is a vivid example of the sacramental principle. The ordained
minister is a visible sign of the invisible presence of Jesus
Christ. Frail and human as they are, the ordained are called
to represent Jesus Christ to their people. They are to pursue a
life of holiness and be willing to sacrifice their own comfort
and convenience for the sake of their people's spiritual good.

They are to devote themselves to the study of Scripture, so that they can proclaim the word of God with power and conviction. Above all, they need to be in prayerful communion with Christ, so that their ministry will flow from him rather than from themselves.

When people think about what is distinctive about Catholicism, they easily think of the sacraments. No other religion, I would venture to say, takes the material world more seriously. Catholics believe that in the simple actions and words of the seven sacraments, Jesus Christ becomes present and acts within the souls of believers to nourish and strengthen their relationship with him. The sacraments do not act like magic. The believer must approach them with faith and with the desire to receive what Christ wants to give us. For those who do, the sacraments are times of personal encounter with the One who came that we might have life in abundance (John 10:10).

Finally, we need to say a word about how certain we can be of our salvation. The way Catholics understand biblical teaching, we can have a firm hope of salvation, but not absolute assurance. The Bible gives many indications that even committed believers have the potential to slip away from fidelity to God; therefore, we need what Catholics call "the grace of final perseverance." Some examples from Scripture include the following:

In talking about the last days, Jesus says there will be a host of physical and moral evils coming upon the world, so that believers will be severely tested: "And because of the increase of lawlessness," he says, "the love of many will grow cold. But the one who perseveres to the end will be saved" (Matthew 24:12-13).

- St. Paul writes: "Work out your own salvation with fear and trembling" (Philippians 2:12). Why would

Paul say that if our salvation were absolutely assured through our belonging to Christ? I have often wondered how fundamentalists deal with that statement.

- Paul himself did not claim absolute certainty about his salvation. In one passage he compares the Christian life to a race, although the prize is nothing less than eternal life. Paul even makes this remarkable statement: "I do not run aimlessly, nor do I box as though beating the air; but I punish my body and enslave it, so that after proclaiming to others, I myself should not be disqualified" (1 Corinthians 9:26-27).

I really like what Alan Schreck has to say about the topic of salvation in his excellent book *Catholic and Christian*. He says that a Catholic should be able to give a triple answer to those who ask, "Are you saved?" First, he writes, we can say, "Yes, I *have been* saved. It is an objective fact that Jesus Christ has died and risen to save me from my sins. This salvation has already begun to take effect in the life of everyone who has accepted Christ and received baptism." Second, a Catholic needs to say, "I am *being* saved. I am still running the race to my final destiny in heaven. I have to turn to God each day for the grace to enter into God's plan for my life and to accept God's gift of salvation more fully." And third, a Catholic can say, "I *hope* to be saved. I have to persevere in my faith in God, in my love for God, and in obedience to God's will until the end of my life. I have confidence that God will give me that grace, and that I will accept the gift of salvation until the day I die. Yet I am always conscious of my human frailty and my need for forgiveness and healing."

As someone has pointed out, fundamentalist Protestants seem to confuse salvation with justification. That is, we are *justified* (made righteous) with God when we acknowledge

Jesus Christ as our Lord and Savior and receive him into our hearts. But *salvation* is an ongoing, life-long process of conversion, struggle, backsliding, recommitment, seeking forgiveness, and overcoming our sinful tendencies. And always, always we know that we are not alone: "I am with you always," Jesus said, "to the end of the age" (Matthew 28:20).

III. The Second Coming of Christ

A final issue in the question of salvation concerns the Second Coming of Christ. People have often noted how preoccupied fundamentalists seem to be with the end of the world. They scrutinize the Book of Revelation and believe they can find all sorts of clear indications that the end of the world is imminent. This gives added fervor to their evangelizing efforts: They want to save as many people as possible before it is too late.

Fundamentalists will talk a good deal about what they call "The Rapture" (although the term itself is found nowhere in Scripture). The Rapture in turn is connected with "the millennium," when Christ is supposed to return with his saints to rule over the world for a thousand-year period. The amazing popularity of the recent *Left Behind* series of novels is indicative of the heightened interest in these themes.

Fundamentalists believe that they find this teaching in Revelation 20:2-6, which speaks of Satan being bound up "for a thousand years" and the saints reigning with Christ for that time. Present-day Christians, then, are living in the "pre-millennium," the time just preceding the millennium. This "pre-millennialist" theology is summarized very clearly by Kathleen Boone in her book *The Bible Tells Them So*:

Pre-milliennialists believe the literal, historical deterioration of the earth will culminate in a seven-year period of tribulation, the horrific details of which are culled from the books of Daniel and Revelation. The tribulation, an outpouring of divine wrath and judgment, will close with the Second Coming of Christ, who will then reign on earth during the millennium. Believers, however, will not suffer through the tribulation.

In an event termed The Rapture, Christ will return to gather his saints from the earth immediately prior to the onset of the tribulation. They will return with Christ to reign with him on earth during the millennium.... The Last Judgment occurs with the close of the millennium, with all persons sent to their respective eternal destinations.

It is not difficult to see the implications of this theology. Fundamentalists can find both fear and comfort in it. On the one hand, it is frightening to think about the horrors and disasters that will afflict the earth during the tribulation; on the other hand, it is comforting to think that being one of "the saved" will allow you to be "raptured out" of the tribulation and enjoy a peaceful reign with the Lord.

The other implication has to do with how we spend our time on this earth. If the world is inevitably headed toward moral deterioration and eventual destruction, it is futile to spend our energy in trying to reform it. Rather, we should devote all our efforts to bringing others to make their decision for Christ, so that they will be ready for The Rapture. This is why, for example, Jerry Falwell once said, "Paul did not get sidetracked into social reform. One cannot transform a lost society. The Gospel will transform individuals in society, and this is the minister's calling."

And evangelist Bob Jones has told his flock: "The church is not in the world to bring peace. The Gospel is a sharp, two-edged sword. Christ's commission to his disciples is to preach the Gospel.... The church is not told to change the moral climate of the world. The commission of the church is to save men and women out of the world. Anyone who knows and believes the Scripture recognizes that the moral situation of the world is going to grow worse and worse as we go further and further into the apostasy."

Nevertheless, fundamentalists do not seem to follow this theology consistently. Logically, we would expect them to maintain a posture of distance and non-involvement in political and social concerns, as their verbal rhetoric indicates. Yet Jerry Falwell founded the "Moral Majority," specifically intended to "change the moral climate of the world." Pat Robertson has a clear political agenda and was even a candidate for the presidency. Other fundamentalist leaders urge their followers to oppose legislation that does not reflect Christian values. There seems to be some sort of disconnect here.

In any event, Catholics have quite a different understanding of their role in the world and their attitude toward the future coming of Christ. They believe that Jesus will surely come at the end of time to judge the whole human race and to establish the definitive reign of God over all human history. But it is clear from Scripture that no one knows the exact time that this will occur. Several times Jesus said things like this to the disciples: "But about that day or hour no one knows.... Beware, keep alert; for you do not know when the time will come.... What I say to you I say to all: Keep awake" (Mark 13:32, 33, 37). From the context it is clear that Jesus is speaking both of our individual "hour" (our death) and the "great tribulation" that will precede the end of the world. These momentous events may occur at any time, so we always need to be prepared.

As for the millennium, most Catholic and mainline Protestant biblical scholars do not believe that "the thousand years" in Revelation 20 should be taken literally. Rather, it refers to a long period of time during which Christians will experience a great deal of peace and freedom, a time when Satan's power is bound up and the teachings and influence of Jesus seem to hold sway in the world. Perhaps this period has already taken place, as in the fourth century when the persecutions ceased and most of the Roman Empire became Christian. Or perhaps it is still to come.

At any rate, scholars see no evidence for a rapture or for a literal thousand-year reign of believers together with Christ. As a matter of fact, Revelation 20:4 says that those who are to reign with Christ are those who have already died. There is nothing about the living being "raptured out." St. Paul does speak of those who are alive being "caught up in the clouds together with (the dead) to meet the Lord in the air" (1 Thessalonians 4:17), but he is obviously talking about the final coming of Christ at the end of time.

> *Catholic teaching has consistently maintained that believers are called to be involved and concerned about the state of the world.*

Meanwhile, Catholic teaching has consistently maintained that believers are called to be involved and concerned about the state of the world. This theme is abundantly clear in the Bible. In Matthew 25:31-46, Jesus tells us we will be judged by the way we have responded to our brothers and sisters in need. In the parable of Lazarus, the rich man was sent to hell not because he was rich, but because he had no concern for the poor man at his doorstep (Luke 16:19-31). And in the parable of the talents, the man with the one talent is condemned by his master not because he had only one, but because he did nothing with it (Matthew 25:14-30).

It seems evident that Jesus is telling us that we are responsible for one another's well-being, physical as well as spiritual. Because people have to live in society, we need to take care that the society will be supportive rather than destructive of its members' material and spiritual good. Peter wrote to the early Christians: "Serve one another with whatever gift each of you has received" (1 Peter 4:10).

This notion of Christians as "good stewards" of the earth and its people is a major theme in Catholic social teaching. More than one hundred years ago (1891), Pope Leo XIII wrote his great encyclical *Rerum Novarum* (*On the Condition of Workers*). There he set forth clear principles for our involvement in the building of a just and peaceful world that the Second Vatican Council reiterated: "They are mistaken who, knowing that we have here no abiding city but seek one which is to come (Hebrews 13:14), think that they may therefore shirk their earthly responsibilities" (*Pastoral Constitution on the Church in the Modern World*, n. 43).

Note how careful the bishops are not to split our spiritual life from our temporal life. Later in that same text they say very forcefully that there must be "no false opposition between professional and social activities on the one part, and religious life on the other. Christians who neglect their temporal duties are also neglecting their duties toward their neighbor and even God, and jeopardize their eternal salvation." Those are strong words indeed. They ask us to take this world very seriously, because it is God's handiwork and it is the arena in which we are to grow in holiness and find our salvation.

Our final destiny is heaven, but we are not to "stand there looking up toward heaven," as the angels said to the first apostles in Acts 1:11. Nor do we withdraw from the world because it seems to be getting more corrupt all the time. Rather, we devote our energies to sharing the Good News about Jesus Christ and working to bring about his reign in our world—a wonderful vocation indeed.

Perhaps a brief word is in order here about fundamentalist Catholics in regard to the Bible and to the process of salvation. When it comes to the Bible, fundamentalist Catholics can distort the meaning of Scripture to accommodate their own biases and agendas. Like their Protestant counterparts, they tend toward biblical literalism, especially in matters like evolution. Sometimes, too, they seem overly preoccupied with the themes of "spiritual warfare" and the end-times. But for the most part they share a common understanding and reverence for Scripture along with other Catholics.

Regarding salvation, they hold closely to mainstream Catholic views on the necessity of faith in Jesus Christ, baptism and the other sacraments, and the importance of keeping the commandments and practicing the works of justice and mercy. As mentioned earlier, they tend to stress devotional practices and to put a great deal of emphasis on reports of miracles, private revelations, and the like. They are very zealous in opposing abortion, to the point where they sometimes judge other people and politicians based on this single issue. They even seem suspicious about "the seamless garment" view of the right to life, which includes opposition not only to abortion but also to capital punishment, war, and economic injustice toward the poor. As a result, they sometimes attack other pro-life Catholics who may not show the same passion about abortion.

I have chosen in this chapter not to respond to the fundamentalist Muslim view of salvation. As we saw earlier, all observant Muslims hold to "the five pillars" outlined in a previous chapter: professing faith in Allah as the One God; prayer five times a day; fasting during the holy month of Ramadan; giving alms to the poor; and the pilgrimage to Mecca. We also noted that fundamentalist Muslims seek to impose strict Islamic law on all believers, including restrictions on women, dress codes, physical punishments for crimes, and the like. For them, the surest way to salvation (Paradise) is to establish a Muslim religious state that will strictly enforce Islamic law and forbid the practice of all other religions. But this view is opposed by moderate Muslims who only desire the freedom to live their beliefs alongside others who may be of different faiths.

Salvation and Non-Christian Faiths

Because this book is aimed primarily at a Catholic audience, there is one question that needs to be addressed: If salvation comes through faith in Jesus Christ, how can people of other religions (or no religion) be saved? This is a very serious theological issue that all Christians have to face. Fundamentalist Protestants generally give a simple answer: Such people (Jews, Muslims, Buddhists, pagans, etc.) cannot be saved unless they come to profess faith in Christ. Catholic fundamentalists usually agree with this viewpoint. This is what gives urgency and energy to the evangelism of both

> *If salvation comes through faith in Jesus Christ, how can people of other religions (or no religion) be saved?*

groups—their strong desire to convert as many as possible to Christianity. Of course, such a view seems narrow-minded and intolerant to many people and gives a negative image to fundamentalism.

Mainline Catholics have also wrestled with this question. It was an especially acute issue at the Second Vatican Council when the bishops were trying to adopt a new spirit of openness to all of humanity. On the one hand, they had to maintain the traditional belief that Jesus came to save all people. But on the other hand, what about those many who will never hear about Christ? Or if they do, are not convinced that they must put their faith in him? Does God have some plan also for their salvation?

The council addressed this question head-on in one of its first decrees: *The Dogmatic Constitution on the Church.* After an earnest acknowledgement that devout Protestant Christians as well as Jews can find salvation if they are faithful to their own beliefs, the text goes on to say (I want to quote it at length, since it is so helpful for our understanding):

> But the plan of salvation also includes those who acknowledge the Creator, in the first place amongst whom are the Muslims: these profess to hold the faith of Abraham, and together with us they adore the one, merciful God, mankind's judge on the last day. Nor is God remote from those who in shadows and images seek the unknown God, since...the Savior wills all to be saved (1 Timothy 2:4). Those who, through no fault of their own, do not know the Gospel of Christ or his Church, but who nevertheless seek God with a sincere heart and, moved by grace, try in their actions to do his will as they know it through the dictates of their conscience—those too may achieve eternal salvation. Nor shall divine providence deny the assistance necessary for salvation to those who, without any fault of theirs, have not yet arrived at an explicit knowledge of God, and who, not without grace, strive to lead a good life (n. 16).

This is a refreshing, inclusive view of salvation. It does not negate the centrality of Jesus Christ or the necessity of proclaiming the Gospel to all nations (missionary activity), because, left to themselves, humans too easily fall prey to their own selfish interests or to the immoral standards of the prevailing culture. As Pope Paul VI stated: Every person has a right to at least hear the Christian Gospel, and the Church has the corresponding duty to proclaim it. But the response of the hearers must be free, not coerced in any way. Non-Christians who faithfully observe the tenets of their religion, and non-religious persons who sincerely follow the dictates of their own conscience, can be saved.

Conclusion

"Are you saved?" It is a powerful question, one that perhaps is too readily ignored by contemporary people who think they have more important things to worry about: looking good, getting ahead, being healthy, enjoying "the good life." We are indebted to fundamentalist Protestants for forcing this question into the limelight. But as Catholics we believe that reading the Bible and committing our life to Jesus Christ is too simplistic an answer. We also need to be faithful in keeping God's commandments and practicing the works of justice and mercy. We need to work together with all people of good will to take care of God's creation, to insure that those who are poor and disadvantaged will be able to live in decency and dignity, and that all nations will come together to renounce violence and live in mutual peace. Moreover, because we are weak and inclined to sin and self-indulgence, we need the saving actions of Jesus in the sacraments to help us live our vocation to holiness and to reach our final destination in the life of heaven.

WHAT CATHOLICS CAN LEARN FROM FUNDAMENTALISTS

In this chapter, I will focus primarily on what mainline Catholics can learn and take away from Protestant fundamentalism, as that form of fundamentalism is drawing many Catholics away from the Church. One example of this is Willow Creek Community Church in northern Illinois. It claims that about seventy percent of their members are former Roman Catholics. Other fundamentalist churches report about fifty percent. This has to be matter of deep concern for Catholics. But instead of wringing our hands or trying to fix blame, we would do much better to ask ourselves why this is happening and, even more important, what can we learn from these churches.

First, it is not difficult to understand the appeal of the fundamentalist churches. Their members find profound peace and liberation in their belief system. Whatever doubts they may have had about the future of the economy, or their health, or the condition of the world, they have absolute certainty about the one thing that matters: their eternal salvation. They know they are going to heaven.

Another appealing aspect of fundamentalism is that its members generally appear to embody traditional and family-oriented values. Many members project a positive, cheerful attitude toward life. They are warm and friendly, often the first ones to offer help in time of need. If you are a stranger at their church services or social gatherings, you will be warmly welcomed, introduced to everyone, and made to feel at home. For many Catholics, this is in sharp contrast to what they have experienced in the large impersonal settings of their own parish churches. On college campuses, fundamentalist students are clean-cut and outgoing, have high moral standards, and still know how to have a good time.

Moreover, fundamentalists are encouraged and trained to

be evangelizers. They consider it their mission to go out and save others for Christ. For some curious reason they seem especially anxious to convert Catholics. Perhaps they perceive us as the most deceived and blinded of all Christians. Many Catholics, of course, resent it when fundamentalists persist in asking them "Do you know the Lord?" or "Have you been born again?" Still, it is hard not to admire that kind of zeal and courage, or to wonder why it is not more prevalent in the Catholic Church. Finally, part of the fundamentalist appeal is its simplicity. Just read the Bible and take it literally; commit your life personally to Christ; and attend church regularly. Of course, as members become more involved in the church, they find that more will be asked of them. They are expected to tithe, to be involved in some ministry, and to win others to Christ. I have often wondered: Is one reason we are losing so many members the fact that we do not ask or expect *enough* of our own people?

How Parishes Can Respond

As noted earlier, one of the attractive features of Protestant fundamentalism is its emphasis on the Bible. Some Catholics say they do not find this sufficiently in their own church. What can be done to offset this perception?

For one thing, we who share the preaching ministry need to dedicate our energies to solid biblical preaching. People are hungry for the word of God. It is not enough just to repeat the Scripture texts that were read during Mass and make a couple of obvious applications to life. We have to dig into the text, ponder it, wrestle with it, pray over it until it seeps into our bones. Then we make connections between the sacred text and the lives of our people.

We may shake our heads in dismay over the simplistic way the fundamentalist preachers make use of Scripture. But they have one thing that many of us seem to lack: passion for the Word of God. People are touched and moved by solid, passionate biblical preaching. I usually take the Bible or the Sunday missal into my hands while preaching, so I can easily find and read from the text when I want to. Also, I no longer like to stand behind the pulpit while preaching; I want to move about freely with a portable microphone. I want to do whatever I can to make the word of God come alive in the hearts of my hearers.

Another area in which Catholics need to continue focusing is Bible study. This is the one adult education program that seems to be the most successful in parishes. It is encouraging to see that Bible study has become more common; but there are still too many parishes where it is nonexistent or, if it is in place, it takes the form of an intellectual "head trip" instead of a search for deeper faith and commitment. Nowadays there are a number of excellent Bible study programs in video or DVD format that combine solid teaching along with a process for group reflection and sharing of faith. At the same time, we must not slip into the "Bible-only" mentality of fundamentalists. As we saw earlier, we Catholics have always linked the Scriptures together with tradition and Church teaching for a wholistic understanding of our faith.

Linked with Bible study is a need for ongoing faith formation for adults. Here again, we have to admire the fundamentalist churches for their convictions: They expect members to not only participate in Sunday worship, but also to return on Wednesday evenings for teaching-and-learning sessions. They want their people to be well equipped to both know and share their faith with others. One reason Catholics succumb so easily to the evangelizing efforts of fundamentalists is that many of them have such a meager understanding of their own faith. They take it for granted that they must keep up with the latest developments in their profession: They read the literature in their field, attend seminars, take courses. But when it comes to their religious faith, their knowledge too often remains at the elementary or high school level. Pastors and faith formation directors often complain that they offer high quality educational opportunities, but only a handful of people show up.

One promising development is the recent movement toward "whole-community catechesis." That is, when religious education classes are held for children, parents and other adults are urged to attend at the same time. Together they are given a presentation on some aspect of the faith, with appropriate references to the Bible and *The Catechism of the Catholic Church*. Then the children go with their respective age groups and the adults meet separately to discuss the topic in greater depth. At the end, all come together for a closing prayer service. A couple positive advantages of this approach: first, children and parents are learning together; and second, adults are going deeper in the understanding of their faith.

Another strength of fundamentalists is their stress on having a personal relationship with Jesus Christ. For them, Jesus is not only their Savior but also their friend. They are not satisfied with a "heady" religion, but seek out one that appeals to the heart. Catholics, on the other hand, sometimes feel that their religion is too impersonal, intellectual or ritualistic. They are attracted by the fundamentalists' appeal to "commit your life to the Lord Jesus." As we have seen, this can sometimes be an escape from the hard moral demands of the Gospel. Still, it strikes a responsive chord in the hearts of many Catholics.

I will never forget a statement I once heard from a Catholic prelate, Bishop Raymond Lucker. He said, "Too many Catholics have been catechized and sacramentalized, but not evangelized. They have never formed a personal relationship with Jesus Christ. And I don't blame them," he said. "We taught them for years that you become a Catholic by learning a set of truths and observing a set of rules. But we never taught them to know the Lord."

At its best, the Catholic tradition has tried to place the personal relationship with Christ at the center of religion and spirituality. The goal of the Christian is union with God through Jesus Christ. In the Gospel, Jesus says it clearly: "I am the way, and the truth, and the life. No one comes to the Father except through me. If you know me, you will know my Father.... They who have my commandments and keep them are those who love me; and those who love me will be loved by my Father, and I will love them and reveal myself to them" (John 14:6-7, 21). Note the stress on the intimate, personal relationship between Jesus and the individual, as well as his insistence that love is revealed in action (keeping the commandments), not merely in good feelings.

> *Something else we can surely learn from the fundamentalists is the importance of being a warm and welcoming parish community.*

It may be that we in the Catholic Church have lost some of that deep sense of personal relationship with Christ. We have been preoccupied with revising the liturgy, changing Church structures to include greater lay participation, and motivating people to get involved in social justice issues. These are all necessary, but we always have to take care that we do not lose our center.

Something else we can surely learn from the fundamentalists is the importance of being a warm and welcoming parish community. I was once having lunch with a priest friend in a crowded restaurant on a Sunday noon. He and I were both in retreat ministry at the time, so we were "talking shop" about preaching, prayer leadership, and so on. At the table next to us was a young couple with two beautiful children, and I could see they were straining to hear our conversation. Finally they came over and said, "Excuse us, but we can't help overhearing your discussion. Are you preachers?" "Yes," we said, "we're Catholic priests." They went on to say, "We've just been to church at the Assembly of God. Our pastor is so good. He keeps telling us we need to confess our sins. And we have Bible study every week. And now he wants to build a school so our children can have a good Christian education. Isn't that wonderful?"

We assured them it was, and then they let us know that they "used to be Catholics." Finally I spoke up: "Tell me something. You say you once were Catholic, and now you're moved by the need to confess your sins. Well, we've always had confession in the Catholic Church. We've always had schools for our children, and lately most parishes have begun Bible study. Tell me, what are you finding in your church now that was missing in the Catholic Church?"

Their answer surprised me by its simplicity: "The Catholic Church was so cold!" they said. "Nobody talks to you, nobody smiles, and they'd just as soon run you over when they drive out of the parking lot after Mass. At our church, everyone smiles and says, 'Hi! Welcome! Have you met our pastor—we'll introduce you. Have you heard about our new program for...?'"

I knew what they were saying, and I felt sad. With a little attempt at warmth and welcome, we might still have had this family with us. I've heard enough stories like this to realize this couple is not unique. The good news is that there is nothing to prevent our parishes from becoming more hospitable. In a society where people are constantly on the move, it is becoming more and more imperative that newcomers be welcomed and helped to feel at home in the parish community. Moreover, hospitality should not be limited only to families. As the number of single people increases, it is urgent that our parishes become places of warmth and welcome for all.

One final point in this regard: Catholics sometimes complain that their parish is too large and impersonal and that they do not find a sense of community there. Yet many fundamentalists belong to mega-churches with tens of thousands of members. The difference is that these mega-churches are divided into small groups that meet regularly for faith sharing, to offer support for personal-and-family problems, and for prayer. These small groups meet the human need for intimacy and community, while the larger church body gives a sense of belonging to something grander with a larger purpose and mission. There is no reason why our Catholic parishes cannot create a similar dynamic. Indeed, a number of larger parishes have already moved toward fostering small group communities to meet this need.

What We Can Learn
from Catholic Fundamentalists

One of the chief contributions of Catholic fundamentalists is their call to a stronger and clearer sense of Catholic identity. They claim, with some justification, that the lines of difference between Catholics and other Christians have blurred. As a result, many no longer have a clear understanding of what it means to be Catholic.

In response, Catholic fundamentalist scholars have researched and popularized the writings of the early Fathers of the Church, showing how Catholic beliefs are rooted in long historical tradition. Furthermore, Catholic fundamentalists have developed a renewed interest in apologetics and have provided ordinary Catholics with knowledge and tools to help them explain and defend Catholic teachings to non-Catholics. They have also published catechetical materials for religious education programs that they believe will provide students with a clearer sense of Catholic identity as well as a deeper appreciation of their Catholic faith. In some places they have established new Catholic elementary and high schools (as well as colleges) staffed by religious and laity who have a firm commitment to handing on the faith of the Church as taught by the magisterium. Sometimes, however, these efforts take on the hard edge of intolerance and near-arrogance that we have identified as the dark side of fundamentalism.

Catholic fundamentalists have also worked to revive what used to be called "popular devotions." Many in the post-Vatican II Church abandoned these because they wanted to restore the centrality of the Mass—surely a worthy goal. But now there is a sense that the Eucharistic liturgy alone is not meeting all the spiritual needs of Catholics. So fundamentalists are moving to restore some devotional practices like Holy Hours, adoration of the Blessed Sacrament, scriptural prayer services centered on the Sacred Heart of Jesus or on the life of Mary, or on healing for our personal hurts and family problems. Some parishes are already experimenting with forms of devotional prayer and find that these are satisfying a real hunger in many people. They can tie Catholics back to their devotional roots and provide a sense of spiritual identity. However, if these practices are not rooted firmly in Scripture and in solid Catholic theology, they can degenerate into maudlin sentimentality and individualistic piety.

Undoubtedly, the recent permission from the pope to allow the Latin Tridentine Mass will be welcomed by fundamentalist Catholics as another way to foster their spiritual growth. There is, however, a danger that these practices may create a two-tiered Catholicism made up of those who follow the "orthodox" way of belief and practice, and those who are seen as somehow "on the liberal fringe." We need to keep firmly in mind that the Catholic Church has wide arms, capable of including diverse groups within its embrace.

Catholic Responses to Islam

Because of immigration there can be little doubt that in the next few decades Catholics will have increasing contact with various groups of Muslims. It is crucial that Catholics be aware that there is nearly as much diversity among Muslims as there is among Christians. Hopefully, known terrorists will be denied entry into this country, so we can reasonably assume that the Muslims we meet have come to the United States for the same reasons our own ancestors came: to find work, to raise families, and to practice their religion in freedom. Consistent with our theology and spirituality, we will be called upon to respect them as persons and to refrain from any form of discrimination in regard to housing, employment, and the like.

But more is possible. We can make efforts to learn about their religion, not only to understand but also to appreciate their beliefs and practices. It is good, for example, to remember that Muslims believe, as we do, in the one God who is Creator and Lord of the entire universe. Moreover, they trace their religious roots back to Abraham, since their Arab ancestors descended from Abraham's first son, Ishmael. Muslims also honor Jesus Christ as a great prophet and Mary as his virgin mother.

On the other hand, we need not tolerate the attempts of some Muslims to forcibly convert Christians or to malign Jews. We expect the same degree of tolerance and respect from them as they can expect from us. In a word, we should try to live peacefully with people of different religious and ethnic backgrounds.

At the same time, we should be willing to share our Catholic beliefs and practices with Muslim co-workers, neighbors, or students who show interest. If some have become secularized and abandoned their Islamic faith, they may even be open to conversion to Catholicism.

How to React When a Loved One Becomes a Fundamentalist

I would like to offer a few thoughts for those Catholics whose family members or friends have joined Protestant fundamentalist churches. In fact, the advice in the following pages could be easily applied to love ones who become Islamic or Catholic fundamentalists. In the first place, whatever else you do, continue to love them. Do not reject or disown them no matter how hostile they may become. In some extreme cases, of course, you may have to forbid them to enter your home if they are upsetting or pressuring your own children. But continue to pray for them and to treat them lovingly. At the same time, do not blame yourself for their leaving the Church. In all likelihood, you provided them with a solid Catholic education and your own good example. You could not protect them from all the other influences they were exposed to, and they made their own decisions when they became adults. They alone are responsible for their choices.

Second, try to affirm whatever good you see happening in their lives through their involvement in a fundamentalist church. Sometimes it will be obvious that they are becoming more prayerful, more faith-filled, more devoted to God and to Jesus Christ. Perhaps they have become more responsible, more conscientious as parents. They may seem genuinely filled with joy and peace. It would be wrong to "knock" any of this just because they found it outside the Catholic Church. I often hear parents say, "Father, they are such good kids!" Right.

On the other hand, do not hesitate to challenge what you see as objectionable or inconsistent with true Christian principles. As I mentioned in the first chapter, fundamentalist believers can sometimes be almost cruel in their self-righteousness and intolerance of others. These and other unloving behaviors are surely out of place in one who claims to be a follower of Jesus. Sometimes, too, you may be able to show them how they are becoming unbalanced: for example, giving so much time and energy to their church that their own children's needs are being neglected, or perhaps it is evident that they are becoming joyless, grim and restricted.

Finally, try to avoid getting into arguments with them about the Bible—what someone called "biblical shoot-outs." For one thing, you will never win; they can always come back with another Scripture quote to confound you. For another, you will probably never succeed in convincing them so long as they are in an argumentative frame of mind. What you can do, though, is ask them some provocative questions or give them some Scripture quotes and just ask them to think about them. I have already indicated a number of these biblical issues in the chapter called "Sacred Books." Here are some suggestions:

- Why do you think that your interpretation of that Scripture passage is the only correct one? Who is your authority?

- On what grounds do you reject the Eucharist when Jesus says so plainly that "unless you eat the flesh of the Son of Man and drink his blood, you have no life in you" (John 6:53)?

- Why do you insist that good works are useless when the Bible says, "What good is it, my brothers and sisters, if you say you have faith but do not have works? Can faith save you?" (James 2:14).

Your friends or family members may come back with a quick answer they have learned in their churches; still, such questions can be thought-provoking. And if they ever reach a point at which they want to know more about what we believe, or if they really have a question they want you to answer, assure them that you will track it down and share it with them. As Peter wrote, "Always be ready to make your defense to anyone who demands from you an accounting for the hope that is in you; yet do it with gentleness and reverence" (1 Peter 3:15-16).

It is always painful to watch those we love rejecting the religious beliefs and values we have tried so hard to teach them. And it is especially difficult when we feel powerless to do anything. Here is where, I believe, we need to grow in trust. If we sincerely tried our best, with the insights we had at the time, to give our loved ones a firm grounding in the Catholic faith, then we can entrust them to God with full confidence. Their spiritual welfare is now in God's hands. What more can be asked of us than that we pray for them, give them a good example of Christian living, and continue to love them? God surely desires their salvation even more than we do. May all of us—Catholics, Protestants, Muslims—continue to seek the Lord in sincerity of heart.

Inter-Religious Dialogue

While it may seem that religious groups have become more discordant, it is heartening to note some recent attempts to reduce the tension and hostility between religions. There have been any number of conferences where Christians and Muslims present their similarities and differences in a spirit of mutual respect and desire to learn from one another. The same is happening between Catholics and Evangelical Protestants. In April of 2002, for example, there was a conference of scholars representing the two groups. It was held at Wheaton College (an Evangelical stronghold) and attracted some 400 participants. It became evident that the two traditions, despite some major theological differences, share much common ground. Both are strongly committed to pro-life positions and to family values. Both are committed to the central doctrines of the Trinity, the Incarnation, the saving death and bodily resurrection of Jesus. And both are strong on the mission of the churches to evangelize both individuals and the wider culture without attempting to impose Christian beliefs on anyone or to create a Christian theocracy. These examples of ecumenical dialogue are certainly signs of the work of the Holy Spirit in our time.

A final note in this regard: Quite recently (October of 2007) 138 senior Muslim leaders from around the world sent a letter to Pope Benedict XVI and other Christian leaders proposing that the theological similarities between the two religions ought to be a basis for peace and understanding. The letter held up two similarities found in both the Qu'ran and the New Testament: belief in one God and love of neighbor.

French Cardinal Jean-Louis Nauran, president of the Pontifical Council for Interreligious Dialogue, told Vatican Radio that the letter is "a very encouraging sign because it demonstrates that good will and dialogue are capable of overcoming prejudices." He went on to say that all religious leaders must call on their followers to affirm "the three convictions contained in the letter: that there is one God; that God loves us and we must love God; and that God calls us to love our neighbor."

Never before have Muslims delivered this kind of definitive consensus on Christianity. Rather than engage in polemic, the signatories have adopted the traditional and mainstream Islamic position of respecting the Christian Scriptures and calling on Christians to be more, not less, faithful to them.

Catholic Evangelization?

It may seem that Protestant fundamentalists have appropriated evangelization as their exclusive domain, but it is an essential part of Catholic doctrine as well. In this connection, there is something else we can catch from the fundamentalist churches: their evangelizing spirit. Many Catholics are confused and even intimidated by the word evangelization. It calls up images of front-door arguments with Jehovah's Witnesses, Bible-toting televangelists, and radio preachers telling listeners how wrong Catholics are. At the very least, most Catholics are put off by the thought of trying to convert their non-Catholic friends or co-workers. Much of the negative reaction stems from confusing the idea of evangelizing with *proselytizing*, which uses heavy-handed tactics to persuade others that their beliefs are wrong and ours are right—and therefore, they had better join us.

That is not what we are talking about. Evangelizing simply means sharing with others our beliefs about Jesus Christ and inviting them to take a look for themselves. Our purpose is not to "make everyone Catholic"; rather, it is to be obedient to the command of Jesus to "Go into all the world and proclaim the Good News to the whole creation" (Mark 16:15; also Matthew 28:18-20).

Think of the early Christians. They lived their newfound faith with joy and enthusiasm. Soon their Jewish or pagan friend would say, "You've changed—what happened to you?" The new Christian would say, "You're right; I've come to know Jesus Christ." And the friend would say, "Well, tell me about him." So the Christian would tell the story of Jesus; and if the friend was touched by God's grace, he or she might say, "That's what I'm looking for—how can I find it?" And the Christian would say, "I'll introduce you to the leaders and the catechumens; there you can learn all about us."

That's how the Christian faith spread. There were not a lot of mass conversions; rather, there were many one-to-one connections between people. That's why St. Paul so often praised the early Christians for the fact that "the word of the Lord has sounded forth from you" (1 Thessalonians 1:8), and that their faith was being talked about everywhere. Clearly these Christians were not just keeping the faith; they were spreading it, and Paul was proud of them.

I think one reason we Catholics have been reluctant to evangelize in our own time is that we were not given much encouragement to do so. We've come to think that our religion is pretty much a private matter, "something between God and me." Yet, as long ago as 1975, Pope Paul VI wrote a powerful encyclical, *On Evangelization in the Modern World*. In it he reminded Catholics that evangelization is the Church's "primary and essential mission." That's pretty strong language. He also declared that it is the task of every baptized member, not just the bishops and priests. "It is unthinkable," he wrote, "that a person should accept the Word (of God)...without becoming a person who also bears witness to it and proclaims it in turn" (n. 24).

Then in the 1990's, the bishops of the United States realized that Catholics as a whole were not responding to the call to evangelize, largely because they did not understand the meaning of evangelization and lacked the skills and confidence to actually do it. So in 1992 the bishops published their national pastoral plan for evangelization entitled *Go and Make Disciples*. In it they present an attractive vision of evangelization based on Scripture and on the deepest needs of human persons. One of the goals they set forth is to create in all Catholics a joy and enthusiasm for their faith so that they will be eager to share it with others. In particular, they hope that the laity will be willing to reach out in love to Catholics who are no longer practicing their faith, as well as to those who belong to no church community. The message should not be, "Come and join us or you'll end up in hell," but rather, "We care about you. You are welcome here, and we believe you will find a true spiritual home with us."

We are not bent on trying to persuade believing, committed members of other faiths to become Catholics (sometimes called "sheep-stealing"). Rather, our concern is for those vast numbers of people in our own environment who are spiritual-

ly lost and perhaps searching, often unconsciously, for something to believe in. Many of them are baptized Catholics who
no longer practice their faith; countless others are without any
church connection whatever. Jesus once referred to himself as
"the good shepherd" who does not wait for the straying sheep
to return to the fold, but goes out personally in search of them
(John 10:14-16).

Research has shown that many of these people would like
to connect or reconnect with a church community, but they
are reluctant to make the first move. If someone would simply
reach out to them in genuine friendship, lend them a listen-
ing ear, and invite them to take a new or first look at our
Catholic community, they might well respond. It is not enough
to continue investing all our energies in "saving the saved"
or maintaining the status quo. There are so many people we
are simply not reaching, and we need to become proactive on
their behalf. As a Church we need to become mission-driven
rather than maintenance-driven.

Over the past twenty-five years I have been working in
evangelization ministry in several different dioceses. One approach I have used is to conduct a training course for lay people on how to evangelize one-to-one. I call it "How to Share
Your Faith Without Being Obnoxious." I also call it "kitchen-
table" or "workplace" evangelizing, because it can be used
practically anywhere—in the home, at work, in the restaurant
or bar, over the telephone. The idea is that when people open
up to us about the problems or stresses in their lives, we can
be trained to be good listeners. Then, when we sense it is the
right moment, we can direct the conversation to the spiritual
level. We can tell them about a time in our own life when we
went through something similar, and we experienced God's
help in a very wonderful way. We can ask them where they are
in their own relationship with God. We can offer to pray with
them, right there. We may invite them to pray, or come with us

to Mass or to our Bible study group, or to take whatever step they may be ready for in their spiritual journey.

I am convinced that if we ask, God will show us when and how to evangelize and will give us the courage to do it. It is gratifying to see how people actually begin using these simple skills and gain confidence that they can really be effective evangelists.

But it is also important that the whole parish develop an evangelizing mentality. This can be done through the Sunday homilies, prayers of intercession for inactive Catholics and the unchurched, bulletin inserts about evangelization, and the like. Bible study and prayer groups can take on an evangelizing focus. The parish can create programs of outreach to hurting and disaffected Catholics. Parishioners can be trained to call or visit every household as a way to reach the many who are not walking with us. Eventually every parish committee and organization begins asking itself, "How are we evangelizing? How are we being obedient to the command of Jesus to bring his Good News to everyone in this environment?"

Perhaps we Catholics have been so preoccupied with getting our own house in order (especially in the wake of the clergy sex abuse scandals) that we have not caught the fire that our popes and bishops are trying to kindle in us. Certainly, it would be self-defeating to invite people into a parish that is divided into factions, or is cold and lifeless. On the other hand, we cannot wait until the parish becomes perfect before we begin evangelizing. My experience has been that when parishes do begin to evangelize, the other dimensions and concerns of parish life also become energized.

Affirming Our Catholic Faith

Sometimes, when Catholics are challenged by fundamentalists, they begin to wonder (maybe for the first time in their lives): Why am I a Catholic? Why do I remain a Catholic? These are good questions to ask, and everyone will have to answer for themselves. Let me share with you my own answers to those questions, based on my own convictions as well as on the testimony I have heard from other practicing Catholics.

One aspect of Catholicism that appeals to many is its historical roots. By that I mean that the Catholic Church is able to trace itself back to the time of Christ and the apostles. It gives us a deep sense of continuity to know that we are spiritually connected, through our common faith and the Communion of Saints, with Peter and Paul, Mary the mother of Jesus, the early martyrs, and all the saintly men and women who were nurtured in the Church. In spite of violent opposition and persecution, and even in spite of its own sins and scandals, this Church has endured to the present day. This can be explained, we believe, only by the divine guidance of the Holy Spirit.

Not only has the Church endured—it has grown and spread to all parts of the world, just as Jesus said it would (see Matthew 24:14). The word "catholic" literally means "universal." The Church has always taken seriously Jesus' command to proclaim the Gospel to all nations. This accounts for its evangelization and its missionary spirit. People have often noted that no matter where they may be traveling in the world, they can always find a Catholic church.

This connects with another aspect of the Church that Catholics find appealing: the Church manages to preserve unity amid all this diversity. A danger in any religious movement is that it will splinter when the founder and first disciples are no longer around. Members begin to disagree on teachings and practices, and before long the camps split up. We noted earlier that, since the time of Luther, the Protestant churches have divided into more than 35,000 different branches. We saw that there is a need for some kind of divinely guided authority to ensure that disputes do not become divisions. Catholics believe that Jesus provided for this when he said: "You are

Peter, and on this rock I will build my church, and the gates of Hades will not prevail against it. I will give you the keys (a biblical symbol of authority, see Isaiah 22:22) of the kingdom of heaven; and whatever you bind on earth will be bound in heaven, and whatever you loose will be loosed in heaven" (Matthew 16:18-19). Jesus entrusted Peter and the other apostles and their successors (popes and bishops) with the authority needed to preserve unity in the Church. In another place he said to the apostles, "Whoever listens to you listens to me, and whoever rejects you rejects me, and whoever rejects me rejects the one who sent me" (Luke 10:16). And he promised that they will be guided, not by their own lights, but by the light of the Holy Spirit: "When the Spirit of truth comes, he will guide you into all the truth" (John 16:13).

> *In spite of violent opposition and persecution, and even in spite of its own sins and scandals, this Church has endured to the present day. This can be explained, we believe, only by the divine guidance of the Holy Spirit.*

At the same time, this authority must not become so heavy-handed that it stifles legitimate differences and imposes an artificial conformity. In my experience, Catholics who choose to remain in the Church do so because they find a basic unity on essential issues, along with a healthy sense of freedom and room for different viewpoints and expressions of faith.

Let me mention one final strength that many Catholics find in their Church: a sense of care and compassion for those who are suffering. They find that the Church is there for them in times of hurt and pain, loss and grief, anxiety and guilt. Of course, the Catholic Church has no monopoly on compassion. And sometimes the Church seems more stern and judgmental than compassionate. Whenever that happens, it drives people away. But most Catholics believe that, over the long haul, the Church has a fairly good record of caring for people's needs. In times of crisis and social upheaval, the Church has tried to direct its resources toward the alleviation of human suffering. The result has been a steady commitment to the works of mercy: the founding of schools and academies, hospitals and nurseries, shelters and meal programs.

Moreover, the Church has struggled to address the causes of human misery, even in the face of criticism and opposition. Recent popes—John XXIII, Paul VI, John Paul II, and now Benedict XVI—have been tireless in their defense of human rights and political freedom. In many parts of the world today, the Catholic Church is the only voice of protest against the exploitation of the poor and the brutal violence of oppressive governments. In the United States, the Catholic bishops have spoken out forcefully for the rights of the unborn, for the end of capital punishment, for the elimination of nuclear weapons, and for restructuring the economy so that it does not work systematically against the poor and minority citizens.

Certainly, the Church still falls short of what Jesus intended it to be. It has lagged behind the secular society in affirming equal rights for people of color and for women. It has tolerated clergy who used their position to enrich themselves and gratify their own ego. It has persecuted and even put to death people of other faiths. It has denounced and harassed some of its own members who were calling for reform. For these reasons, the Second Vatican Council declared that the Church "is at the same time holy and sinful, ever in need of repentance and renewal." And John Paul II, in his encyclical at the beginning of the new millennium, said candidly that the Church must humbly confess its own sinfulness, "recalling all those times in history when [Christians] departed from the spirit of Christ and his Gospel and…indulged in ways of thinking and acting which were truly forms of counter-witness and scandal." Not only confess, the pope said, but also to "make amends [for these sins] and earnestly to beseech Christ's forgiveness" (nn. 33-35).

And yet, despite all its flaws and mistakes, the Church in every age has produced women and men who were models of holiness and examples of Christian living for all the faithful. Some have been declared saints, but most have not. Their lives have been convincing truth of the power of the Gospel to transform ordinary people and make them "the good fragrance of Christ" (2 Corinthians 2:15) in the midst of a troubled world. In a way, the Church's history is much like the people, clergy and lay, in every parish in the world: an embodiment of good and evil, sin and holiness. Jesus once compared the kingdom of God to a field in which both wheat and weeds grow together. This does not mean the Church should be complacent about its defects. The worst weeds can and should be uprooted. But the Church will never be perfect. And we do not belong to the Church because we are good or holy; we belong and participate precisely because we are sinners and needy and weak and imperfect. As someone once put it, "The Church is not so much a mansion for saints as a hospital for sinners." Still, the saints in our midst are an inspiration and a reminder of what we all can become with the grace of God.

CONCLUSION

If I could summarize what I have been saying in one sentence, I might put it this way. For me and for many people I know, being Catholic means trying to hold together what should not be separated: Scripture and tradition; faith and works; Bible and sacraments; authority and freedom; unity and diversity; personal salvation and concern for social justice. In any case, it is not enough to be a Catholic simply because one was brought up that way. Each of us needs to think it through and make a personal decision.

Perhaps that is a major difference between Catholicism and fundamentalism (whether Protestant, Muslim, or Catholic): the importance of using our reason and intelligence to understand and live out our faith. Fundamentalists too easily tend to embrace without critical thought a few sacred texts, or a small set of doctrines and rules, or a number of slogans, and then make these the total content of their belief system. For Catholics, reason and faith work together to help us find answers to the great questions of life. And, at the end of the day, Catholics know that they have to leave room for mystery. God and God's ways are so vast, so far beyond our human comprehension, that we can only stand in awe and exclaim with St. Paul, "O the depth of the riches and wisdom and knowledge of God!" (Romans 11:33).

SOURCES AND SUGGESTIONS FOR FURTHER READING

Catholic Evangelization

DeSiano, Frank & Boyack, Kenneth. *Creating the Evangelizing Parish* (Mahwah, Paulist Press, 1993).

Pable, Martin, OFM Cap. *Reclaim the Fire* (Notre Dame, Ave Maria Press, 2002. Book is of print, but can be obtained from the author at mpable@sarcenter.com).

Catholicism

Camille, Alice. *Invitation to Catholicism* (Skokie, ACTA Publications, 2001).

Invitation to the Old Testament (Skokie, ACTA Publications, 2004).

Invitation to the New Testament (Skokie, ACTA Publications, 2004).

Catholic Answers Staff. *The Essential Catholic Survivor Guide* (San Diego, Catholic Answers, 2005).

Farrell, Melvin, SJ, and McHugh, Joseph. *Getting to Know the Bible* (Skokie, ACTA Publications, 2003).

Mahon, Leo. *Jesus and His Message* (Skokie, ACTA Publications, 2000).

Keating, Karl. *Catholicism and Fundamentalism* (San Francisco, Ignatius Press, 1988).

Pable, Martin, OFM Cap. *Remaining Catholic: Six Good Reasons for Staying in an Imperfect Church* (Skokie, ACTA Publications, 2005).

Schreck, Alan. *Catholic and Christian* (Ann Arbor, Servant Books, 1984).

Islam

Armstrong, Karen. *Islam: A Short History* (New York, Modern Library, 2002).

Gourley, Bruce. *Islamic Fundamentalism: A Brief Survey Islam* (published online: BruceGourley.com, 2003).

Hotaling, Ed. *Islam Without Illusions* (Syracuse University Press, 2003).

Mark, Clyde. *Islam: A Primer* (Congressional Research Service, 2003, www.opencrs.com/document/RS21432/).

Protestantism

Hart, D.G., *That Old-Times Religion in Modern America: Evangelical Protestantism in the Twentieth Century* (Chicago, Ivan R. Dee, 2003).

McGrath, Alister, *Christianity's Dangerous Idea: The Protestant Revolution—A History from the Sixteenth Century to the Twenty-First* (San Francisco, HarperOne, 2007).

Sweeney, John M., *Born Again and Again: Surprising Gifts of a Fundamentalist Childhood* (Orleans, MA, Paraclete Press, 2005).